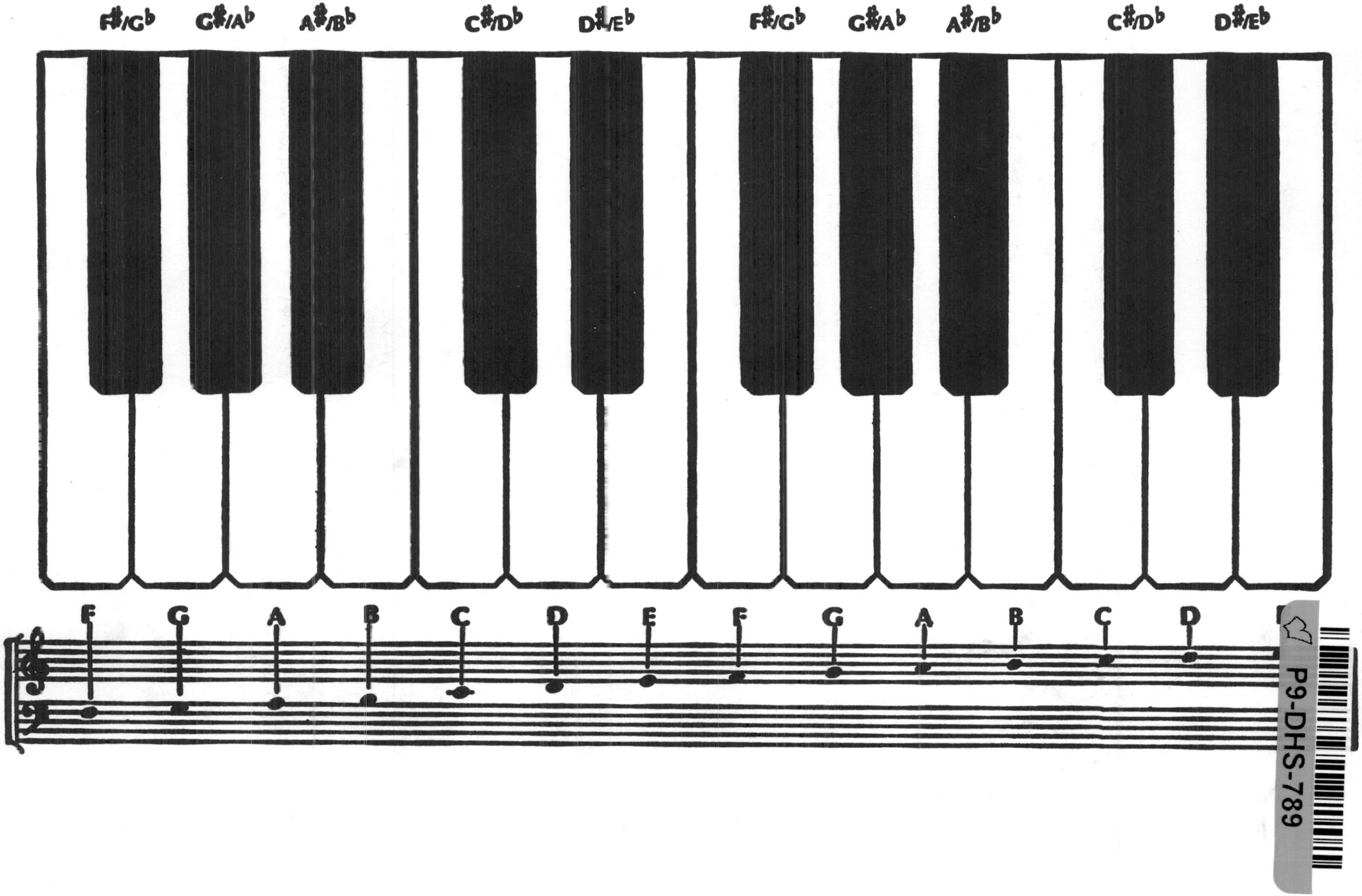
F#/Gb G#/Ab A#/Bb C#/Db D#/Eb F#/Gb G#/Ab A#/Bb C#/Db D#/Eb
F G A B C D E F G A B C D

THE Music CONNECTION
SILVER BURDETT GINN

PROGRAM AUTHORS

Jane Beethovon
Dulce Bohn
Patricia Shehan Campbell
Carmen E. Culp
Jennifer Davidson
Lawrence Eisman
Sandra Longoria Glover
Charlotte Hayes

Martha Hilley
Mary E. Hoffman
Sanna Longden
Hunter March
Bill McCloud
Janet Montgomery
Marvelene Moore
Catherine Nadon-Gabrion

Mary Palmer
Carmino Ravosa
Mary Louise Reilly
Will Schmid
Carol Scott-Kassner
Jean Sinor
Sandra Stauffer
Judith Thomas

RECORDING PRODUCERS

Darrell Bledsoe
Jeanine Levenson

J. Douglas Pummill
Buryl Red, Executive Producer

Linda Twine
Ted Wilson

Scott Foresman

Editorial Offices: Glenview, IL • Parsippany, NJ • New York, NY
Sales Offices: Reading, MA • Duluth, GA • Glenview, IL
Carrollton, TX • Menlo Park, CA

ISBN 0-382-34502-9

8 9 10 - QW - 08 07 06 05 04 03 02 01

C·O·N·T

CONCEPTS 2

UNIT 1	Rhythm	4
2	Rhythm	16
3	Melody	28
4	Harmony	40
5	Melody	52
6	Form	62
7	Rhythm	68
8	Form	78
9	Harmony	88
10	Tone Color	98
11	Tone Color	106

THEMES 112

UNIT 1	We All Live Together	114
2	Music of Our Country	130
3	Just Imagine	152
4	Friends Around the World	166
5	Let Freedom Ring	182
6	Sounds of Fall	192
7	Winter Celebrations	202

THEME MUSICAL
| This Beautiful Land We Share | 224 |

·E·N·T·S

READING.................238

UNIT 1 Review   240
     2 Four Sixteenth Notes   245
     3 Focus on Low *la,* Low *so*   255
     4 Recorder   268
     5 Letter Names   279
     6 Summary   291

REFERENCE BANK

Recorder   302
Sound Bank   304
Glossary   309
Classified Index   311
Song Index   315
Acknowledgments and Picture Credits   317

CONCEPTS

When you listen to music,
you may hear the melody first, or
perhaps the rhythm will catch your attention.
You might notice how different instruments sound,
both alone and together. You might be aware
of other music concepts such as harmony or
form—the way a piece of music is built
from bits and pieces.

This section will connect
you with the concepts of music.

You will sing songs, listen to recorded pieces,
and play instruments to help you learn about each of
these concepts. You will meet famous composers and
hear music they have written. You can move,
dance, and even make up music of your own.

Knowing how the concepts of music work
together often helps people enjoy music more.

section 1

The BEAT Really Counts

In a musical film based on the story *Charlotte's Web*, Charlotte and some other animals sing of ways in which they are alike. These are the things they have in common. What do you have in common with your classmates?

We've Got Lots in Common   from *Charlotte's Web*   CD 1-1, 2

Words and Music by Richard M. Sherman and Robert B. Sherman

1. Oh, we've got lots in com-mon where it real - ly counts,
2., 3. 'Cause we've got

Where it real - ly counts, we've got large a - mounts.

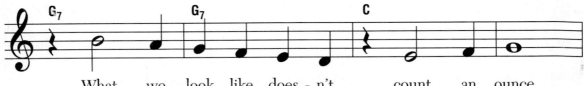

What we look like does - n't count an ounce,

Last time to Coda

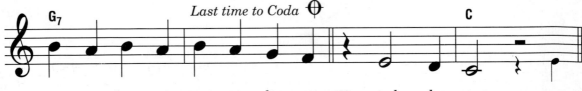

We've got lots in com-mon where it real - ly counts.

(Wilbur) 2. You've

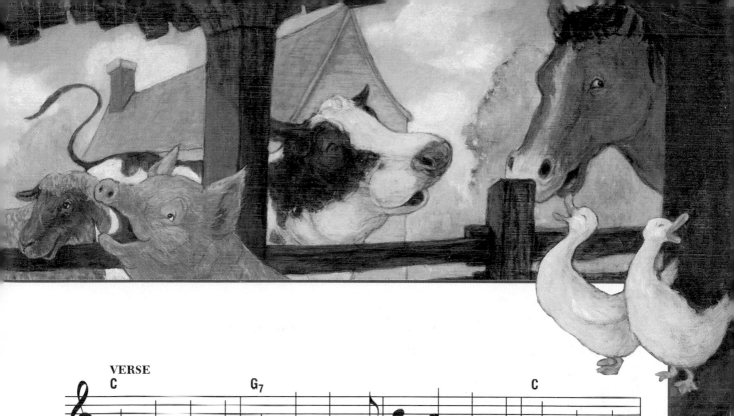

VERSE

(Wilbur) 1. You've got feath-ers, I've got skin, but both our out-sides hold us in.
got a beak and I've a snout, but both of us can sniff a-bout.

(Cow) I've got hooves, you've got webbed feet, but we both stand up to eat,
(Horse) You'll say "quack" and I'll say "neigh," but we're talk-ing ei-ther way,

(Charlotte) 3. You're born to swim and me to spin,
but we all love this world we're in.
We share the sun, the earth, the sky
and that's the reason why
We've all got . . . (D.S.)

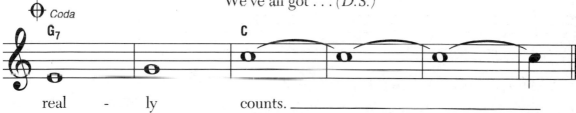

Coda

real - ly counts. _____

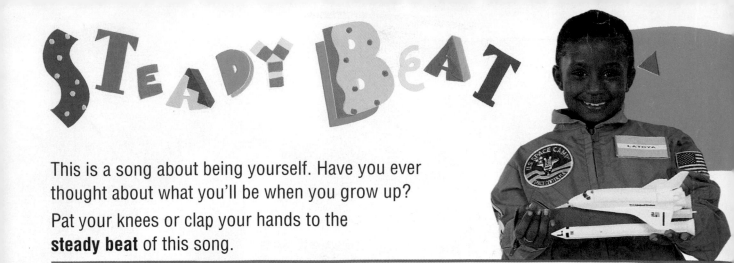

This is a song about being yourself. Have you ever thought about what you'll be when you grow up?

Pat your knees or clap your hands to the **steady beat** of this song.

I Care About Being Me   CD 1-3, 4

Words and Music by Ned Ginsburg and Jeff Sorg

1. I am some-one spe - cial in this great big world, __

There is no one else __ like me. __

I can make a dif - f'rence, make a dream come true, __

'Cause I be-lieve in my-self, _ yes I do. __

REFRAIN

Oh, _____ I care ___ a-bout who I am.

I care ___ a-bout what I do. _____

I care ___ a-bout be-ing the best ___ that I can be,

1.   2.   3.
        D.S.

I care _ a-bout be-ing me. _

2. I can be a doctor or an astronaut,
    All I have to do is choose.
    I can be a farmer with a college degree;
    No one else can decide, only me. *Refrain*

Feel the steady beat as you listen to this piece.

Two-Part Invention No. 8 in F Major

CD 1-5   ....Johann Sebastian Bach

"Rockin' Robin" was a popular hit song in 1958. In 1972, Michael Jackson recorded it and it became a hit again.

Feel the steady beat. How will you move to this music?

CD 1-6, 7

Rockin' Robin

Words and Music by Leon René

1., 3. He rocks in the tree-top all the day long,
2. Ev'ry lit-tle swal-low, ev-'ry chicka-dee,

Hop-pin' and a-bop-pin' and a-sing-in' his song.
Ev-'ry lit-tle bird__ in the tall__ oak tree. The

All the lit-tle birds on Jay-bird Street
wise__ old__ owl, the big black crow,

Love to hear the rob-in go "Tweet, tweet, tweet,"
Flap__ their__ wings,__ singin' "Go, bird, go,"

Rock-in' Rob-in,   Rock-in' Rob-in.

Blow, Rock-in' Rob-in, 'cause we're real-ly gon-na rock to-night. _

2., 3.

A pret-ty lit-tle ra-ven at the bird band-stand

Taught him how to do the bop and it was grand

They start-ed go - in' stead - y, and bless my soul,

D.C. al Fine

He out - bopped the buz-zard and the o - ri - ole.

Listen for the nonsense words in this song.
Can you tap the steady beat?

Do Wah Diddy Diddy
...........Jeff Barry and Ellie Greenwich

CD 1-8

RAPPIN' IN

Do you ever recite rhymes while jumping rope or playing a game? If you do, you are performing a kind of rap. Rap is a style of music that uses words spoken in rhythm.

Listen for these refrains in the recording of *Supermarket Shuffle*.

Supermarket Shuffle
.... Gary Lapow

CD 1-9

1

Supermarket Shuffle
Dancing in the aisle
Supermarket Shuffle
The place gone wild
Supermarket Shuffle
They rock around the clock
You get there in the morning
And it's all cleaned up.

2

Supermarket Shuffle
Bopping on the shelves
Supermarket Shuffle
Nobody gonna tell
Supermarket Shuffle
It's quite informal
You get there in the morning
And it all looks normal.

3

Supermarket Shuffle
Dancing in the aisle
Supermarket Shuffle
The place gone wild
Supermarket Shuffle
They rock around the clock
You get there in the morning
And it's all cleaned up.

Pick a Pattern

Choose one of these rhythm patterns to play or clap while you recite the refrains of *Supermarket Shuffle*.

1.

2.

3.

RHYTHM

4

Supermarket Shuffle
Bouncing to the beat
Supermarket Shuffle
The dairy and the meat
Supermarket Shuffle
Rocking to and fro
You get there in the morning
And you never would know.

5

Supermarket Shuffle
Dancing in the aisle
Supermarket Shuffle
The place gone wild
Supermarket Shuffle
They rock around the clock
You get there in the morning
And it's all cleaned up.

6

Supermarket Shuffle
Bopping on the shelves
Supermarket Shuffle
Nobody gonna tell
Supermarket Shuffle
It's quite informal
You get there in the morning
And it all looks normal.

Write a Rap

Work with a group of your classmates to create your own rap. Then try performing your rap with one of these "rap tracks."

Rap Track 1 ....Joseph Joubert
Rap Track 2 ....Joseph Joubert

CD 1-10, 11

TEMPO:
FAST SLOW

Which pictures show things moving fast?
Which pictures show things moving slow?

Listen to this song. Which part is fast?
Which part is slow?

Stodola Pumpa CD 1-12

Words Adapted by Harry Wilson   *Folk Song from Czechoslovakia*

Ⓐ **VERSE**

1. Come, let us walk a - cross the fields to - day,
2. Back through the fields we'll walk at close of day,

Sing - ing a song as we go on our way,
Stars shin - ing through will light our home-ward way,

Come, let us walk a - cross the fields to - day,
Back through the fields we'll walk at close of day,

Sing - ing a song as we go on our way. ___ Hey!
Stars shin-ing through will light our home-ward way. ___ Hey!

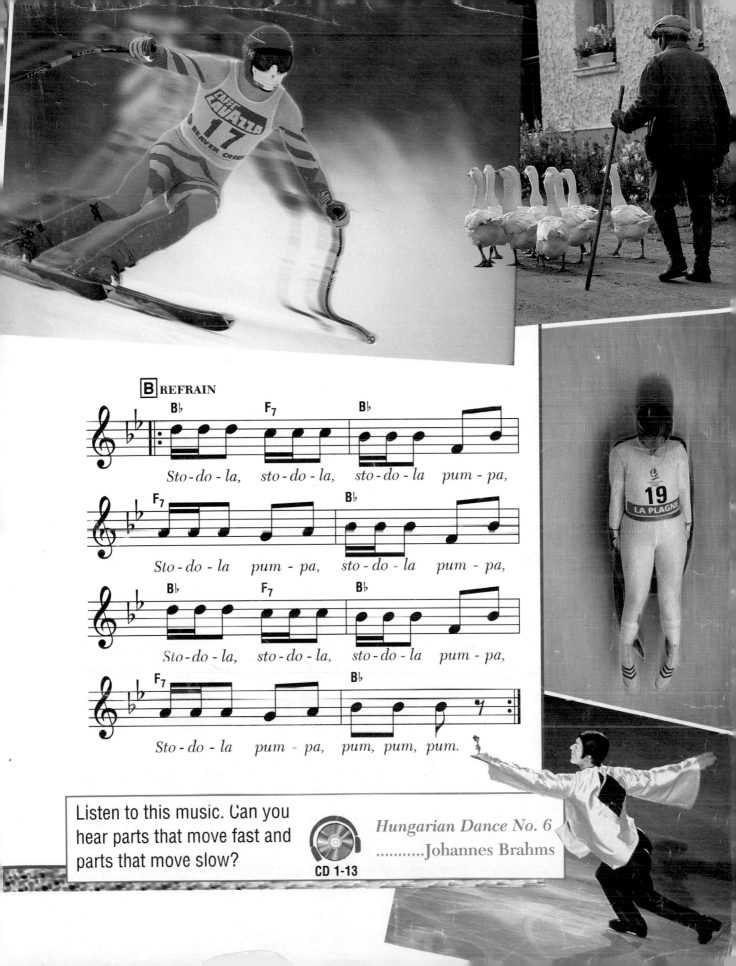

B REFRAIN

Sto-do-la, sto-do-la, sto-do-la pum-pa,

Sto-do-la pum-pa, sto-do-la pum-pa,

Sto-do-la, sto-do-la, sto-do-la pum-pa,

Sto-do-la pum-pa, pum, pum, pum.

Listen to this music. Can you hear parts that move fast and parts that move slow?

CD 1-13

Hungarian Dance No. 6
..........Johannes Brahms

Ragtime Rhythms

Some very special dance rhythms were created by African Americans when they first came to this country. Two famous composers used those rhythms in the pieces you are going to hear.

Maple Leaf Rag by Scott Joplin was published in 1899. It brought success and fame to the composer and is still popular today.

Listen for the beat in this recording of *Maple Leaf Rag*.

Maple Leaf Rag
............Scott Joplin

CD 1-15

Juba Dance by R. Nathaniel Dett is another piece that is still played today. It is based on a dance that was done on plantations that includes foot stamping and clapping.

"Juba Dance"
from *In the Bottoms*
...........R. Nathaniel Dett

CD 1-16

Here are the rhythm patterns that you hear at the beginning of *Maple Leaf Rag*. Can you tell what instrument is playing?

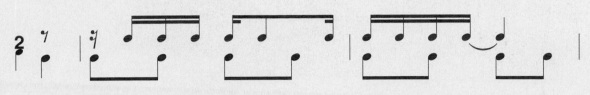

MEET THE COMPOSER

Scott Joplin   (1868–1917)

Scott Joplin was raised in Texarkana, Texas. His father played the violin for plantation dances during the time of slavery. His mother sang and played the banjo. Showing musical talent at an early age, young Scott taught himself how to play the piano. Later he learned to play the cornet and studied composition. Joplin learned to play ragtime style in small cafes. The first publisher he went to with *Maple Leaf Rag* turned it down. But it was finally published and became a bestseller. Joplin wrote more than 50 rags and has been called "the King of Ragtime."

SETS OF TWO

Let your hands "walk" left-right, left-right as you listen to "It's a Small World." Sing along with the music when you can.

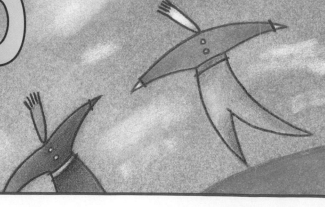

It's a Small World   CD 1-17, 18

Words and Music by Richard M. Sherman and Robert B. Sherman

1. It's a world of laugh - ter, a world of tears,
2. There is just one moon and one gold - en sun,

It's a world of hopes and a world of fears.
And a smile means friend - ship to ev - 'ry one.

There's so much that we share, and it's time we're a - ware,
Though the moun - tains di - vide and the o - ceans are wide,

It's a small world af - ter all.

Which row of symbols shows the steady beat? Which row shows the beats in sets of two?

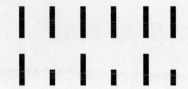

Feel how the music moves in sets of two in this piece.

CD 1-19

East/West

..........Tickle Tune Typhoon

REFRAIN

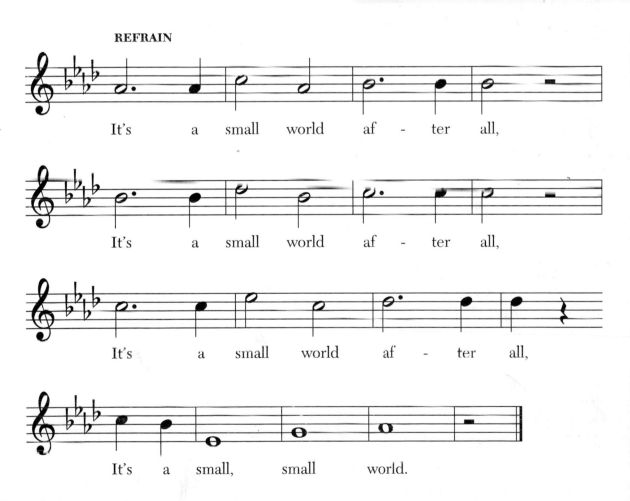

It's   a   small   world   af - ter   all,

It's   a   small   world   af - ter   all,

It's   a   small   world   af - ter   all,

It's   a   small,   small   world.

SETS OF THREE

As you sing "I've Gotta Crow," feel how the music moves in sets of three.

I've Gotta Crow from *Peter Pan*

Words by Carolyn Leigh   Music by Mark Charlap   **CD 1-20**

(Crowing sounds)

I've got - ta crow! (er er er er _____)
I've got - ta brag. (er er er er _____)

I'm just the clev - er - est fel - low 'twas ev - er my for - tune to know.
I think it's sweet I have fin - gers and feet I can wig - gle and wag.

(er er er er _____) I taught a trick to my shad - ow
(er er er er _____) I can climb trees and play tag with

to stick to the tip of my toe,
the breeze in the mead - ow be - low,

I've got - ta crow! _____

If I were a ver - y or - di - nar - y ev - 'ry - day thing,

Listen for the sets of three in this song.

"Worlds Apart" from *Big River*
................Roger Miller

I'd nev-er be heard cock-a-doo-dl-ing 'round like a bird!

(That's ab - surd!) (er er er)

But, nat - u - ral - ly, (er er er er_____)

When I dis - cov - er the clev - er - ness of a re mark - a - ble me,

(er er er er_____) How can I hide it when deep down in - side

it just tick - les me so_____

that I've got - ta let go_____ and crow!_____

Meter in 2

Pretend to strum a banjo as you listen to this song. Feel the beats moving in sets of two. This is also called **meter in 2**.

What sign tells you that this song moves in meter in 2?

Boil Them Cabbage Down

CD 1-22

Pioneer Song from the United States

1. The rac-coon's got a fur - ry tail,

The 'pos-sum's tail is bare, —

The rab-bit ain't got no tail at all,

But a lit-tle bit o' bunch o' hair.

From MORE SONGS OF THE NEW WORLD by Desmond MacMahon.
Published by Holmes McDougall Ltd.

Steady Beat—Strong Beat

Play the steady beat on a woodblock.

Play the strong beat on a tambourine.

Does the music move in meter in 2
or in meter in 3 in this listening piece?

"March" from *Nutcracker Suite*
..............Piotr I. Tchaikovsky

CD 1-23

B REFRAIN

Boil them cab-bage down, down, Bake them bis-cuits brown, brown,

The on-ly tune I ev-er did learn is Boil them cab-bage down.

2. The June bug he has wings of gold,
   The firefly wings of flame,
   The bedbug's got no wings at all,
   But he gets there just the same. *Refrain*

3. Oh, love it is a killing fit
   When beauty hits a blossom,
   And if you want your finger bit,
   Just poke it at a 'possum. *Refrain*

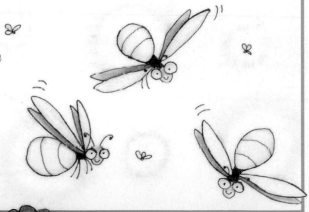

METER IN 3

The top row of pennants shows the steady beat. What does the bottom row show?

Take Me Out to the Ball Game

CD 1-24

Words by Jack Norworth   Music by Albert von Tilzer

Take me out to the ball game,

Take me out with the crowd. ___

Buy me some pea - nuts and crack - er - jack,

I don't care if we nev - er get back.

Pick a Pattern

Which pattern will you use to accompany the song?

Woodblock

Drum

Tambourine

Let me root, root, root for the home team,

If they don't win it's a shame, ____

For it's one, two, three strikes you're out

At the old ball game. ____

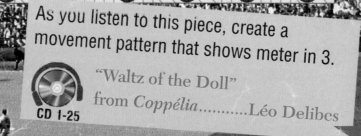

As you listen to this piece, create a movement pattern that shows meter in 3.

CD 1-25   "Waltz of the Doll" from *Coppélia*...........Léo Delibes

Coffee Grows in 3 and 2

People danced to this American folk song many years ago. You can sing it and learn the dance, too.

Coffee Grows on White Oak Trees   CD 1-26

Folk Song from the United States

REFRAIN

Cof - fee grows on white oak trees.

The riv - er flows with hon - ey - o.

Go choose some - one to roam with you,

As sweet as m'las - ses can - dy - o.

Which part of this song moves in meter in 3? Pat your hands on your *knees* when the music moves in threes.

Can you find the part of the song that moves in meter in 2? Clap your hands when the music moves in twos.

1. Two in the mid - dle and they can't go o - ver,

Two in the mid - dle and they can't go o - ver,

Two in the mid - dle and they can't go o - ver,

Hel - lo, Su - san Brown.

2. Swing you another one and you'll get over,   *(3 times)*
   Hello, Susan Brown.   *Refrain*

3. Four in the middle and they all go over,   *(3 times)*
   Hello, Susan Brown.   *Refrain*

Ballet Music

Nutcracker Suite, by Piotr I. Tchaikovsky, is music written for a ballet, a kind of dance that often tells a story. A ballet is usually performed on a stage, with costumes and scenery. Men, women, and children dance in this ballet.

Listen to two of the dances from *Nutcracker Suite.* One moves in meter in 3, the other in meter in 2. Can you tell which is which?

CD 1-27

"Dance of the Reed Flutes"
from *Nutcracker Suite*
.............Piotr I. Tchaikovsky

CD 1-28

"Arab Dance"
from *Nutcracker Suite*
.............Piotr I. Tchaikovsky

Melodies from "Dance of the Reed Flutes"

Three flutes play the first melody.

A trumpet plays a contrasting melody.

MEET THE COMPOSER

Piotr Ilyich Tchaikovsky was born in Votkinsk, a little village in eastern Russia. From his earliest childhood, Piotr's main interest was music. But there were no concerts in Votkinsk, so most of Piotr's music came from a music box that his father had brought from St. Petersburg. Piotr would sit for hours listening to its tunes. As soon as he was big enough to sit at the piano, he began to make up tunes of his own.

Tchaikovsky composed a great deal of music. Today, more than 100 years after his death, Tchaikovsky's beautiful melodies are heard in concert halls all over the world.

Piotr Ilyich Tchaikovsky   (1840–1893)

REPEATED TONES

Look at the notes in the color box. Do they move upward or downward, or do they stay the same?

Follow the music as you listen to the song. Can you find other places where the tones repeat?

Four White Horses

Folk Song from the Caribbean   **CD 1-30**

Four white hors - es on the riv - er,

Hey, _____ hey, _____ hey, _____ up to - mor - row,

Up to - mor - row is a rain - y day.

From 120 SINGING GAMES AND DANCES FOR ELEMENTARY SCHOOL by Lois Choksy & David Brummitt.
Used by permission of the publisher, Prentice-Hall.

What words or phrases repeat in this poem?

No Rain, No Rainbow

Suppose today
you're feeling down,
your face propping a frown;

Suppose today
you're one streak of a shadow,
the sky giving you a headache.

Tomorrow,
you never know,
you might wake up
in the peak of a glow.

If you don't get the rain,
how can you get the rainbow?

Say it again, Granny,
No rain, no rainbow.

Say it again, Granny,
No rain, no rainbow.

—*John Agard*

Come on up ____ to the shal - low bay.

Shal - low bay ____ is a ripe ba - na - na,

Up to - mor - row is a rain - y day.

Upward and Downward

Look at the notes in the blue color box. Do they move upward or downward, or do they stay the same?

Look at the notes in the red color box. How do they move?

Lullaby for the Trees   CD 2-1, 2

Words and Music by Jeanine Levenson

VERSE

1. Come with me to the for - est floor,
2. "Take my gift," says the ap - ple tree.

See how the beau - ty sur - rounds __ you. _____
"Shade from my limbs __ will cool __ you. _____

O - pen wide the __ for - est door,
Climb up high, there's so much to see.

Let the sun shine through. _____
All the world looks new." _____

© 1993 Jeanine Levenson

The Ups and Downs of FRIENDSHIP

The Surprise is the story of two friends, Frog and Toad, who try to help each other. Listen to the story to discover what the surprise is.

CD 2-4

The Surprise ....Arnold Lobel

Look at the notes in the color boxes. Do they move upward or downward? By step or by leap?

Melody 1

It's a beau-ti-ful day to-day. My heart is full of want-ing to help my friend in an - y way. It's a beau-ti-ful day to - day.

Melody 2

Can you find the notes in this melody that move upward? Downward?

I have such a spec - ial friend.

We can do all kinds of things to - geth - er.

Try singing these two melodies together.

May our friend - ship nev - er end.

It's so nice to help a friend you love.

Words by Judith Thomas. Music from Orff-Schulwerk MUSIC FOR CHILDREN VOLUME II, ed. by M. Murray.

Play this accompaniment with the melodies on page 32.

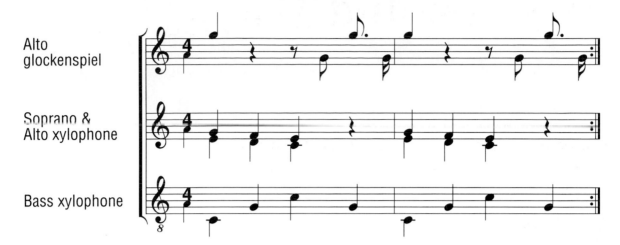

Alto
glockenspiel

Soprano &
Alto xylophone

Bass xylophone

Try to **improvise**, or make up, your own melody. Include a pattern that moves mostly upward or mostly downward. Use these notes: C, D, E, G, A, and C.

Decide how you could use these melodies to add music to the story of *The Surprise*.

TONES MOVE BY LEAP

Look at the notes in the color box. Do they move by step, do they stay the same, or do they leap?

Two Wings   CD 2-6

African American Spiritual

1. Oh, Lord, I want two wings to cov - er ___ my face,
2. I want two gold - en shoes to put on ___ my feet,

Oh, Lord, I want two wings to fly ___ a - way,
I want two gold - en shoes to put on ___ my feet,

Oh, Lord, I want two wings to cov - er ___ my face,
I want two gold - en shoes to put on ___ my feet,

So   the   world   can't   do   me   no   harm. ___
So   the   world   can't   do   me   no   harm. ___

3. I want a golden harp to play by myself,   *(3 times)*
   So the world can't do me no harm.

Does the music move mostly by steps or by leaps in this piece?

"Polka"
from *The Age of Gold Ballet*
..............Dmitri Shostakovich

CD 2-7

Among the greatest gifts to American music are African American spirituals. They have been an important part of our national heritage since the 1800s.

"Two Wings" is a spiritual that tells about wishing for two wings, two golden shoes, and a golden harp. Can you find other examples of African American spirituals in your book?

James Leonard, Wind Machine with Gabriel, Eleanor Roosevelt, and Louis Armstrong, 1984. National Museum of American Art, Washington, D.C./Hemphill Collection/Art Resource, New York.

Wind Machine with Gabriel, Eleanor Roosevelt, and Louis Armstrong   *James Leonard*

A Day to Step, Leap, and Repeat

Can you find the steps, leaps, and repeated tones in this song?

It's a Beautiful Day

CD 2-8, 9

Words and Music by Greg Scelsa

See the sun shin-ing in the win-dow, time to start a new _ day. _

Can't you hear the song-birds sing-in'? Got-ta sing out loud and say _

that it's a beau-ti-ful day _ for run-nin' in the sun,

a beau-ti-ful day _ that's just _ be-gun, _____

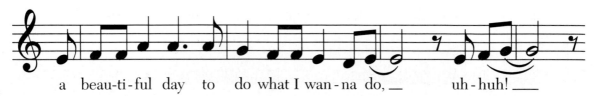

a beau-ti-ful day to do what I wan-na do, _ uh-huh! _

Yes, it's a beau - ti - ful day __ just to be a - live, __

a beau-ti - ful day, __ so glad __ that I've __ got a beau-ti - ful day __

Fine

and I'd like to share it with you. _____

Look a - round, there's a world of beau - ty

from the moun - tains to the sea, __

And there's a won - der 'round __ ev - 'ry cor - ner

D.S. al Fine

a - wait - ing there for you and me. __ Yes, it's a

One Composer, Two Moods

The two pieces you will hear were composed by Robert Schumann. They are among the best-known and best-loved piano pieces of all time. Children play the pieces for family and friends. Famous pianists play the pieces in concert halls all over the world.

As you listen to the music, look at the words in the two lists below. Which list of words suggests the mood, or feeling, of the music in the first piece? In the second piece?

cheerful	quiet
jolly	peaceful
lively	calm

"The Happy Farmer" from *Album for the Young*
CD 2-10 ....Robert Schumann

"Dreaming" from *Scenes from Childhood*
CD 2-11 ....Robert Schumann

Here is the melody you hear at the beginning of *The Happy Farmer*.

You hear this melody at the beginning of *Dreaming*.

MEET THE COMPOSER

Just one year after Abraham Lincoln was born in Kentucky, a baby boy named Robert Schumann was born in a German village near Leipzig, which was at that time a major musical center of the world. Lincoln grew up to be President of the United States; Schumann became one of Germany's finest composers.

Schumann studied piano with Friedrich Wieck, one of the best piano teachers of the day. It was for Wieck's daughter Clara that Schumann wrote *Scenes from Childhood*, a series of 13 piano pieces, including "Traümerei" (which means "dreaming" in German).

Robert Schumann (1810–1856)

Melody AND Harmony

When a song has harmony, two or more different tones sound at the same time.

You will hear two performances of "America." As you listen to the recording, decide which one has harmony and which does not.

America, Two Ways
.........Traditional Melody

CD 2-13

Two Ways to Add Harmony

Add harmony to "Brother John" by playing chords on an autoharp. As the class sings the melody, play the F chord all through the song.

Do you know what an **ostinato** is? An ostinato is a melody or rhythm pattern that repeats throughout a song.

Another way to add harmony to "Brother John" is to sing or play an ostinato. As the class sings the melody, try one of these ostinatos.

Voices or Bells

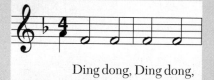

Ding dong, Ding dong,

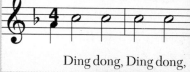

Ding dong, Ding dong,

Bro-ther John,   Bro-ther John,

Brother John CD 2-14

Traditional Round from France

Are you sleep - ing, Are you sleep - ing?

Broth - er John, Broth - er John?

Morn-ing bells are ring - ing, Morn-ing bells are sing - ing,

Ding ding dong, Ding ding dong.

PICK A PARTNER

Listen to these three American folk songs.
Follow the music of each as you listen.
Sing along when you can.

Sandy Land   CD 2-15, 18, 19

Folk Song from Oklahoma

1.   Make my liv-in' in sand - y land,   Make my liv-in' in sand - y land,

Make my liv-in' in sand - y land,   La - dies, fare you well.

2.   Raise sweet potatoes on sandy land, . . .

3.   Dig sweet potatoes in sandy land, . . .

4.   Make my livin' in sandy land, . . .

Putting Two Songs Together

While some of your classmates sing "Sandy Land,"
others can sing "Bow, Belinda" or "Skip to My Lou."

Singing **partner songs** is one way to create harmony.

Bow, Belinda   CD 2-16, 18

Singing Game from the United States

1. Bow, bow, bow, Be - lin - da; Bow, bow, bow, Be - lin - da;

Bow, bow, bow, Be - lin - da; You're the one, my dar - ling.

2. Right hand round, oh, Belinda; . . .

3. Left hand round, oh, Belinda; . . .

4. Both hands round, oh, Belinda; . . .

Skip to My Lou   CD 2-17, 19

Game Song from the United States

1. Flies in the but-ter-milk, shoo, fly, shoo! Flies in the but-ter-milk, shoo, fly, shoo!

Flies in the but-ter-milk, shoo, fly, shoo! Skip to my Lou, my dar - ling.

2. Lost my partner, what'll I do? . . .

3. I'll get another one, that's what I'll do! . . .

4. Flies in the buttermilk, shoo, fly, shoo! . . .

You can add harmony to a song with a melodic ostinato. This song is especially fun because each melody line can be an ostinato.

The Wheel of the Water

Words and Music by John Forster and Tom Chapin   **CD 2-20**

Voice 1

The wheel of the wa - ter go 'round and 'round,

And the wheel of the wa - ter go 'round. And the

Voice 2

Wa - ter flow down, down, trick - le, trick - le down,

© 1990 by John Forster and Tom Chapin, Limousine Music Co. and Sundance Music. Used by permission. All rights reserved.

Can you create a "spoken ostinato"
using words or phrases from this poem?

The Water-Go-Round

Oh, the sea makes the clouds,
   And the clouds make the rain,
And the rain rains down
   On the mighty mountain chain;

Then the silver rivers race
   To the green and easy plain—
Where they hurry, flurry, scurry
   Till they reach the sea again;

And the sea makes the clouds,
   And the clouds make the rain,…

—*Dennis Lee*

Down to the o - cean, trick - le, trick - le down.

Voice 3

See the va - pors rise. See them cloud the skies.

Voice 4

Clouds rain down. Thun - der and light - ning sound.

Voice 5

Springs bub-ble, bub-ble up. Springs bub-ble, bub-ble up.

Rounds! Rounds! Rounds!

Rounds can be spoken. Try this vegetarian round.

‖:Ar-ti-choke, broc-co-li, ru-ta-ba-ga, corn:‖

‖:Ar-ti-choke, broc-co-li, ru-ta-ba-ga, corn:‖

Rounds can be played using your body as a percussion instrument.

Clap
Patsch R
Patsch L
Stamp

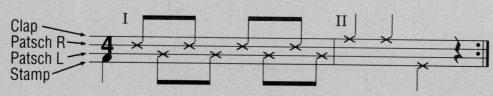

Try playing this round for percussion instruments.

Maracas
Woodblock
Drum

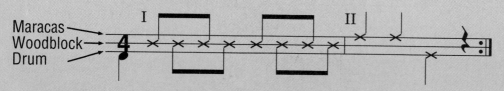

Rounds can also be played on mallet instruments.

From Orff-Schulwerk MUSIC FOR CHILDREN, VOLUME I, ed. by M. Murray.

Can you create a movement round with your classmates?

Round and Round and Round

Listen for the voices playing follow the leader in the recording of this song.

Make New Friends
CD 2-21

Traditional Round

I

Make new friends, but keep __ the __ old, __

II

One is sil - ver and the oth - er gold.

When you and your classmates can sing the melody of "Make New Friends" without the recording, try singing the song as a two-part round.

Listen to a singing group named Sweet Honey in the Rock perform this song.

Make New Friends .... Traditional Round

CD 2-22

Lullaby

This lullaby from *Peter Pan* may be sung as a round.

Tender Shepherd

from *Peter Pan*

Words by Carolyn Leigh   *Music by Mark Charlap*   **CD 2-23**

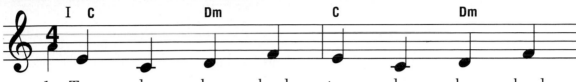

1. Ten - der shep - herd, ten - der shep - herd,
2. Ten - der shep - herd, ten - der shep - herd,

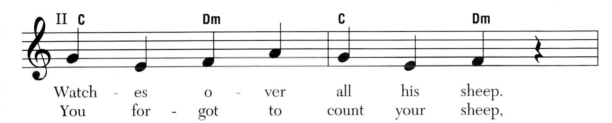

Watch - es o - ver all his sheep.
You for - got to count your sheep,

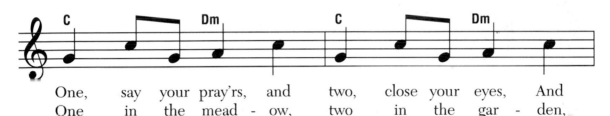

One, say your pray'rs, and two, close your eyes, And
One in the mead - ow, two in the gar - den,

three, safe and hap - pi - ly fall a - sleep.
Three in the nur - ser - y fast a - sleep.

Can you find these notes in "Tender Shepherd"?

Try playing them on the bells to create an introduction for the song.

Choose another pattern that would make a good **coda**, or ending, for the song.

The Firebird

The story that Igor Stravinsky tells in his ballet *The Firebird* is about the adventures of Prince Ivan, hero of many Russian folk tales, and a mysterious bird with flaming feathers. In one part of the story, the firebird lulls 13 beautiful princesses into a magic sleep to protect them from an evil king. Here is the music from that part of the story.

"Berceuse"
from *The Firebird*
.............Igor Stravinsky

CD 2-24

Ostinato Pattern

Here is a melodic ostinato that you hear in "Berceuse."

Listen for this sleepy bassoon melody near the beginning of the piece.

MEET THE COMPOSER

Igor Stravinsky (1882–1971)

Igor Stravinsky was born in Russia. His father was a famous singer at the Russian Imperial Opera. Igor often went to opera rehearsals with his father and learned to love the musical theater when he was still a young boy.

During his lifetime, Stravinsky composed many pieces of music, including several ballets. In addition to *The Firebird*, he wrote *The Rite of Spring* and *Petrouchka,* a ballet about a puppet that comes to life.

Follow the Phrase Lines

Notice the phrase lines above the music. As you listen to the recording, trace each phrase line with your finger.

Whaka Poi CD 2-25, 26

Canoe Dance from New Zealand

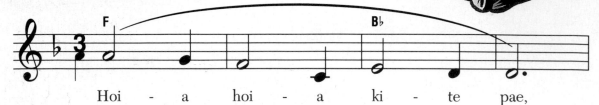

Hoi - a hoi - a ki - te pae,

Hoi - a hoi - a ki - te pae,

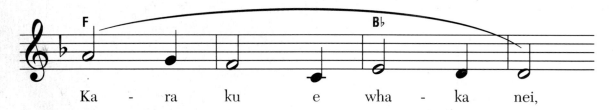

Ka - ra ku e wha - ka nei,

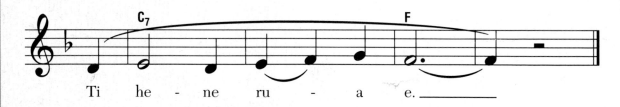

Ti he ne ru - a e. _____

Listen for the phrases in this recording.
How can you move to show the phrases?
CD 2-27

"Soldier's March" from *Album for the Young*
.............Robert Schumann

Learn to perform a canoe dance with "Whaka Poi." The movements show how the oars move in the water.

Phrases
that
Look
Alike

As you listen to the recording, trace the shape of each melodic phrase with your finger. Which phrases sound alike? Do they look alike, too?

Down in the Valley
CD 2-28

Folk Song from Kentucky

1. Down in the val - ley, val - ley so low,
2. Build me a cas - tle for - ty feet high,

Hang your head o - ver, hear the wind blow.
So I can see you as you pass by.

Hear the wind blow, dear, hear the wind blow,
As you ride by, dear, as you ride by,

Hang your head o - ver, hear the wind blow.
So I can see you as you ride by.

3. Writing a letter, containing three lines,
   Answer my question: "Will you be mine?"
   Will you be mine, dear, will you be mine?
   Answer my question: "Will you be mine?"

As you listen to "Peace like a River," trace a phrase line in the air to show each phrase. Trace them from left to right. How many short phrases do you find? How many long phrases?

Peace like a River   CD 2-29, 30

African American Spiritual

1. I've got peace like a riv-er,

I've got peace like a riv-er,

I've got peace like a riv-er in my soul.

I've got peace like a riv-er,

I've got peace like a riv-er,

I've got peace like a riv-er in my soul.

2. I've got joy like a fountain, *(2 times)*
   I've got joy like a fountain in my soul.
   I've got joy like a fountain, *(2 times)*
   I've got joy like a fountain in my soul.

3. I've got love like the ocean, *(2 times)*
   I've got love like the ocean in my soul.
   I've got love like the ocean, *(2 times)*
   I've got love like the ocean in my soul.

A phrase in

As you learn "The Jasmine Flower,"
try singing each phrase on one breath.

The Jasmine Flower   CD 2-31

English Words Adapted by Julia Bingham   *Based on a Folk Melody from China*

1. See __ this branch __ of __ sweet - est __ flow'rs,
2. Take _ this branch __ of __ jas - mine _ flow'rs,

Plucked __ at morn _ from _ dew - y ____ bow'rs;
Plucked __ at morn _ from _ dew - y ____ bow'rs;

Sent with love ___ to greet me,
Given with love ___ to greet you,

Breath - ing friend - ship sweet.
Breath - ing friend - ship sweet.

a Breath

Create a Phrase

Can you create a phrase that can be used as a melodic ostinato for "The Jasmine Flower"? Use any of these notes. Will you use steps? Leaps? Repeated tones? Both steps and leaps?

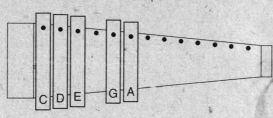

Remember, your melody also needs a rhythm pattern. Choose one of these patterns or create your own.

Tomb Figurines   *Táng Dynasty*

Táng Dynasty (613–906). Tomb Figurines. Glazed earthenware. 8 3/4 inches. Acc. No. 27.191. The Detroit Institute of Arts, Gift of Ton-Ying and Co.

Musical

Netty Simons wrote the music called *Set of Poems for Children* when her own children were young. She used to make up tunes on the piano while reading their favorite poems to them.

Follow the words of "Fog" and "My Shadow" as you listen to the recordings. What happens in the music that makes you think of fog or a shadow?

CD 2-32
"Fog" from *Set of Poems for Children* ....Netty Simons

CD 2-33
"My Shadow" from *Set of Poems for Children* ....Netty Simons

MEET THE COMPOSER

Netty Simons (1913–   )

Netty Simons, an American composer, was born in New York City. She attended New York University and The Juilliard School of Music. She enjoys creating interesting tone colors in all of her music. In addition to her pieces for children, she has written an opera, two ballets, and many instrumental pieces. Her music has been performed in European countries, in Japan, in Australia, and throughout the United States.

Poems

Fog

The fog comes
on little cat feet.

It sits looking
over harbor and city
on silent haunches
and then, moves on.

—Carl Sandburg

My Shadow

I have a little shadow that goes in and out with me,
And what can be the use of him is more than I can see.
He is very, very like me from the heels up to the head;
And I see him jump before me, when I jump into my bed.

The funniest thing about him is the way he likes to grow—
Not at all like proper children, which is always very slow;
For he sometimes shoots up taller like an India-rubber ball,
And he sometimes gets so little that there's none of him at all.

He hasn't got a notion of how children ought to play,
And can only make a fool of me in every sort of way.
He stays so close beside me, he's a coward you can see;
I'd think shame to stick to nursie as that shadow sticks to me!

One morning, very early, before the sun was up,
I rose and found the shining dew on every buttercup;
But my lazy little shadow, like an arrant sleepyhead,
Had stayed at home behind me and was fast asleep in bed.

—Robert Louis Stevenson

Go Two By Two—Ⓐ Ⓑ

The signs Ⓐ and Ⓑ tell you that this song has two different sections. Can you find them in the song?

Ambos a dos   CD 2-35, 36

English Words by Aura Kontra   *Folk Song from Latin America*

Ⓐ **REFRAIN**

Am - bos   a   dos,   ma - ta - ri - le,   ri - le,   ri - le,
Go   two   by   two,   ma - ta - ri - le,   ri - le,   ri - le,

Am - bos   a   dos,   ma - ta - ri - le,   ri - le,   ron.
Go   two   by   two,   ma - ta - ri - le,   ri - le,   ron.

Ⓑ **VERSE**

1.   Yo ten - go un   cas - ti - llo,   ma - ta - ri - le,   ri - le,   ri - le,
1. Come in - to   my   cas - tle,   ma - ta - ri - le,   ri - le,   ri - le,

Yo ten - go un   cas - ti - llo,   ma - ta - ri - le,   ri - le,   ron, pon, pon.
Come in - to   my   cas - tle,   ma - ta - ri - le,   ri - le,   ron, pon, pon.

2. ¿Dónde están las llaves? . . .   2. *Where's the key to the door?* . . .
    ¿Dónde están las llaves? . . .   *Where's the key to the door?* . . .
    Refrain   Refrain

Ⓐ Ⓑ Ⓐ Ⓑ Ⓐ Ⓑ Ⓐ Ⓑ Ⓐ Ⓑ Ⓐ Ⓑ Ⓐ Ⓑ Ⓐ Ⓑ Ⓐ Ⓑ Ⓐ Ⓑ Ⓐ Ⓑ

The game that goes with "Ambos a dos" has different actions for each section of the song.

SING IT AGAIN

Find the musical sign in this song that tells you to sing a section two times.

What do you think the form of this song is?

Little Boy of the Sheep   CD 2-37

English Words by Alice Firgau   *Folk Song from the Hebrides Islands*

A
G   C   G

Sing me a song,   pipe me a tune,

G   Am   D₇   G

Guard the sheep well,   O shep - herd boy.

B G   C

Keep - ing the sheep all   day, watch - ing they   do   not stray

G   D₇   G

O - ver the   hill - side, O shep - herd boy.

Used by permission of Margaret Fay Shaw.

With a group of your classmates, try playing this recorder part while the rest of the class sings the A section of "Little Boy of the Sheep."

Here's a part you can play during the B section.

Using the notes D, E, and G, improvise your own tune to accompany Section B.

Fies a Song in A A BB

The First of January (Uno de enero)

Folk Song from Mexico CD 3-3

A

C

First of the first month, sec-ond of the sec-ond month,
U - no de e - ne - ro, dos de fe - bre - ro,

C   **G7**

Third of the third, and fourth of the fourth;
tres de mar - zo, cua - tro de a - bril,

G7

Fifth of the fifth month, sixth of the sixth month,
cin - co de ma - yo, seis de ju - nio,

G7   **C**

Sev-enth of Ju - ly is San Fer - min.
sie - te de ju - lio, San Fer - mín.

B **C**   **G7**   **C**

La, la, la, la, la, la, la, Tam - bou-rine's brok-en, we can-not play it.
¿Quién ha ro - to la pan-de - re - ta?

C   **G7**   **C**

La, la, la, la, la, la, la, If you broke it, you must re-place it.
El que la ha ro - to la pa - ga - rá.

CALL CHART

Listen for the two different sections in this piece for brass instruments.
The chart will help you hear the form.

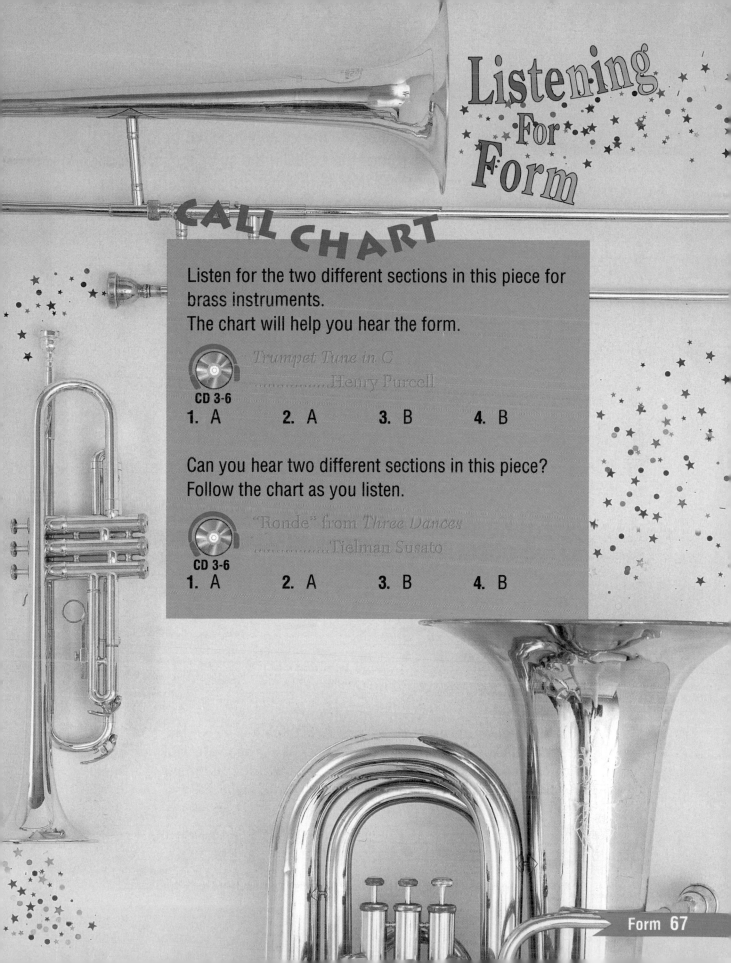

CD 3-6

Trumpet Tune in C
.... Henry Purcell

1. A   **2.** A   **3.** B   **4.** B

Can you hear two different sections in this piece?
Follow the chart as you listen.

CD 3-6

"Ronde" from *Three Dances*
.... Tielman Susato

1. A   **2.** A   **3.** B   **4.** B

Follow the music as you listen to this song. Notice the notes in the color box. Do you hear this rhythm pattern anywhere else in the song?

Billy Boy CD 3-7

Folk Song from England

1. Oh, ___ where have you been, Bil - ly Boy, Bil - ly Boy?
2. Did she bid you to come in, Bil - ly Boy, Bil - ly Boy?
3. Did she give you a chair, Bil - ly Boy, Bil - ly Boy?
4. Can she make a cher - ry pie, Bil - ly Boy, Bil - ly Boy?
5. Can she cook and can she spin, Bil - ly Boy, Bil - ly Boy?
6. How ___ old is ___ she, Bil - ly Boy, Bil - ly Boy?

Oh, ___ where have you been, charm-ing Bil - ly?
Did she bid you to come in, charm-ing Bil - ly?
Did she give you a chair, charm-ing Bil - ly?
Can she make a cher - ry pie, charm-ing Bil - ly?
Can she cook and can she spin, charm-ing Bil - ly?
How ___ old is ___ she, charm-ing Bil - ly?

I have been to seek a wife, She's the joy ___ of my life,
Yes, she bid me to come in, There's a dim - ple in her chin,
Yes she gave ___ me a chair, But there was no bot-tom there,
She can make a cher - ry pie, Quick as a cat can wink her eye,
She can cook and she can spin, She can do most an - y - thing,
Three times six and four times seven, Twen - ty - eight ___ and e - leven,

She's a young thing and can - not leave her moth - er. ___

Chant the *Billy Boy* pattern.   *Bil-ly Boy, Bil-ly Boy, Bil-ly Boy, Bil-ly Boy*

Clap the *Billy Boy* pattern.
Say the words *short-short-long* as you clap.

— — — — — — — — — — — —

Then play the *Billy Boy* pattern on a woodblock.

Can you play these patterns on a woodblock?

1.

2.

3.

Make up a new pattern of short and long sounds. Then work with a group of your classmates to create your own rhythm piece. What instruments will you choose to play your composition?

RHYTHM OF THE MELODY

Look at the notes in the color box. How many places do you see this pattern in the song? Can you clap this rhythm while the class sings the song?

May the Sun Shine Forever   CD 3-8

Russian Words by L. Oshanin   *English Words by Alice Firgau*   *Music by A. Ostrovsky*

May the sun shine for - ev - er,
Pust' 'vse - gda bu - det son - se,

May blue skies be for - ev - er,
Pust' 'vse - gda bu - det nye - ba,

May there ev - er be Ma - ma,
Pust' 'vse - gda bu - det ma - ma,

1. May there ev - er be me!
Pust' 'vse - gda bu - do ya!

2. ev - er be me!
gda bu - do ya!

Rhythms to Play

Try playing the steady beat on the woodblock.

Then choose a different instrument on which to play the rhythm of the melody.

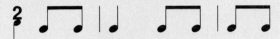

Here is another version of the same song. How is it the same as the song you sang? How is it different?

Let the Sun Shine Forever

..........L. Oshanin and A. Ostrovsky

CD 3-9

Find the Rhythm

As you sing this song, tap the rhythm of the melody.

Turn the Glasses Over

CD 3-10

Folk Song from the United States

I've been to Haar - lem, I've been to Do - ver,

I've trav - eled this wide world all o - ver,

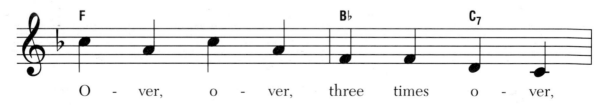

O - ver, o - ver, three times o - ver,

Drink what you have to drink and turn the glass - es o - ver.

Rhythms and Words

Here are some rhythm patterns from this song. Try clapping each rhythm.

Then see if you can find the words in the song that go with each pattern.

Sail - ing east, sail - ing west,

Sail - ing o - ver the o - cean,

Bet - ter watch out when the boat be - gins to rock,

Or you'll lose your girl in the o - cean.

Play a Rhythm

Listen to this conversation between the sun and the moon. How do you think the sun feels about the moon?

The Sun and the Moon *(El sol y la luna)*

English Words by Alice Firgau   Folk Song from Spain   CD 3-13, 14

1. Who is the sun? He's Lo - ren - zo, ti - bi - ton,
1. *El sol se lla - ma Lo - ren - zo, ti - bi - tón,*

And the moon is Ca - ta - li - na. ____
Y la lu - na Ca - ta - li - na. ____

Just be - cause they had a quar - rel,
An - dan siem - pre se - pa - ra - dos

On their sep - 'rate paths now ____ trav - el.
Por dis - gus - tos de fa - mi - lia.

© 1956 Novello & Co. Ltd. from FOLK SONGS OF EUROPE, Ed. by Maud Karpeles.

Choose one of these patterns to play on the claves.

Where do you hear each of these patterns in "The Sun and the Moon"?

REFRAIN

With a ti - bi, ti - bi, ti - bi, ti - bi, ti - bi - ton. ____
Con el ti - bi, ti - bi, ti - bi, ti - bi, ti - bi - tón. ____

With a ti - bi, ti - bi, ti - bi, ti - bi, it is done.
Con el ti - bi, ti - bi, ti - bi, ti - bi, se a - ca - bó.

2. "Moon," said the sun, "You are vain," tibiton,
"Showing off and putting those airs on.
I gave you that dress you're wearing
Just because of my deep caring."   *Refrain*

2. *El sol le dijo a la luna, tibitón,*
   «No presumas demasiado,
   Que el vestido en que luces
   De limosna te lo han dado.»   Refrain

3. "Moon," said the sun, "To be honest," tibiton,
"I no longer wish to see you,
You at night all hours spending
In the streets with bandits, wending."   *Refrain*

3. *El sol le dijo a la luna, tibitón,*
   «No quiero nada contigo;
   Pasas la noche en la calle
   Con ladrones y bandidos.»   Refrain

The Comedians

Dmitri Kabalevsky wrote this music about 50 years ago for a children's play called *Inventors and Comedians*. Later he took some of his pieces about the traveling group of comedians and put them into a suite. (A suite is a collection of pieces organized around a theme.) "March" and "Galop" are two of the pieces.

Listen to "March" and "Galop." How is "Galop" the same as "March"? How is it different?

"March" from *The Comedians*
.............Dmitri Kabalevsky

CD 3-15

"Galop" from *The Comedians*
.............Dmitri Kabalevsky

CD 3-16

A Familiar Rhythm

Try clapping this rhythm. Then play it on a drum.

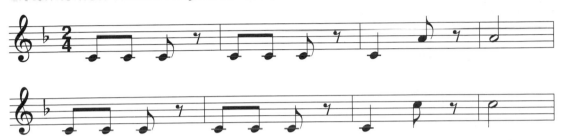

Listen to how Kabalevsky uses this pattern in "March".

MEET THE COMPOSER

Dmitri Kabalevsky was born in St. Petersburg, Russia. When he was a child, he liked to paint and write poetry. He also studied music and became an excellent pianist. By the time he was 21, Kabalevsky was teaching music to children. Some of his first pieces were written especially for his piano students. "March" and "Galop" are two of his most famous selections for children.

Dmitri Kabalevsky (1904–1987)

Kabalevsky is considered to be one of the outstanding Russian composers of the twentieth century.

DISCOVER THE FORM

Listen to the recording of "Now Let Me Fly." Join in singing the A section when you can.

Now Let Me Fly

African American Spiritual **CD 3-17, 18**

A **REFRAIN**

Now let me fly, _____ Now let me fly, _____

Now let me fly ____ way up high, ____

Way in the mid-dle of the air.

Which set of shapes and letters shows the form of "Now Let Me Fly"?

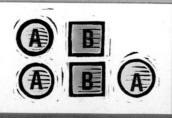

B VERSE

1. Way down yon - der in the mid - dle of the field,

See me work - in' at the char - iot wheel.

Not so par - tic - 'lar 'bout work - in' at the wheel,

D.C. al Fine

But I just wan - na see how the char - iot feels.

2. I got a mother in the Promised Land,
Ain't gonna stop 'til I shake her hand.
Not so partic'lar 'bout shakin' her hand,
But I just wanna get up to the Promised Land.

An ABA Dance

The Loco-Motion
CD 3-19, 20

Words and Music by Gerry Goffin and Carole King

Ev-'ry-bo-dy's do - in' a brand-new dance __ now,
Move a-round the floor __ in a lo - co - mo - tion,

Come on, ba - by, do ___ the lo - co - mo - tion.

I know you'll get to like it if you give it a chance __ now,
Do it hold-in' hands __ if ___ you get the no - tion,

Come on, ba - by, do ___ the lo - co - mo - tion.

This popular song from the 1960s is in ABA form. Work with your classmates to create a movement for the A section and a different movement for the B section.

My lit-tle ba-by sis-ter can do it with ease, —
There's nev-er been a dance — that's so eas-y to do, —

It's eas-i-er than learn-in' your A B C's. —
It e-ven makes you hap-py when you're feel-in' blue. —

Fine

So come on, come on, do — the lo-co-mo-tion with me. —

B

You got-ta swing your hips now, — Come on, ba-by,

D.C. al Fine

Jump up, jump back, Oh, well, I think you got the knack. —

Play a Pattern

Can you find this pattern in the song? Does it occur in the A section or the B section? Can you play the pattern on the bells?

All Night, All Day
CD 3-21

African American Spiritual

REFRAIN
A *Solo*
G

Chorus
C

D₇

All night, all ____ day, An-gels watch-ing o-ver me, my Lord. _

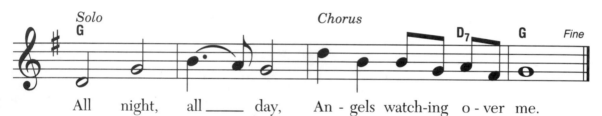

Solo
G

Chorus

D₇ G *Fine*

All night, all ____ day, An-gels watch-ing o-ver me.

VERSE
B *Solo*
G

Chorus
C

D₇

1. Now I lay me down _ to sleep,
2. If I die be-fore _ I wake,

An-gels watch-ing o-ver me, my Lord. _

Solo
G

Chorus

D₇ G *D.C. al Fine*

Pray the Lord my soul _ to keep,
Pray the Lord my soul _ to take,

An-gels watch-ing o-ver me.

Listen for the ABA form in this recording.

Trumpeter's Lullaby
..........Leroy Anderson

CD 3-22

Following the chart will help you hear the AABA form
of this piece for guitar.

 CD 3-23
Adelita ....Francisco Tárrega

1. A   **2.** A   **3.** B   **4.** A

Can you hear the ABA form of this piece for piano?
Follow the chart as you listen.

 CD 3-23
Preludes for Piano, No. 2 ....George Gershwin

1. A   **2.** B   **3.** A

These pictures create a form. What is it?

Dance a Rondo

La raspa
CD 3-24, 25, 26, 27

English Words by Kim Williams   Folk Song from Mexico

How many times do you hear the A section (and its repeat) in "La raspa"?

A

La ras - pa yo bai - lé   al de - re - cho y al re - vés.
The ras - pa I will dance,   as for-ward and back I go.

Si quie - res tú bai - lar,   em - pie - za a mo - ver los pies.
So if you want to dance,   be - gin with your heel and toe.

B

Brin - ca, brin - ca, brin - ca tam - bién,
Al - ways mov - ing, mov - ing your feet,

mue - ve, mue - ve mu - cho los pies.
back and forth now jump to the beat.

Que la ras - pa vas a bai - lar
This is how the dance we will do,

al de - re - cho y al re - vés.
laugh - ing, laugh - ing all the way through.

A
Si quie-res tú bai-lar la ras-pa co-mo yo,
So if you want to dance the ras-pa the way I do,

Me tie-nes que se-guir al de-re-cho y al re-vés.
Be-gin to move your feet, and you will be danc-ing, too.

C *Instrumental*

A
La ras-pa yo bai-lé al de-re-cho y al re-vés.
The ras-pa I will dance, as for-ward and back I go.

Si quie-res tú bai-lar, em-pie-za a mo-ver los pies.
So if you want to dance, be-gin with your heel and toe.

UNDER the BIG TOP

Aaron Copland, an American composer, wrote the music for a movie called *The Red Pony*. The movie is about a ten-year-old boy named Jody, who received a red pony as a gift. Jody loved his pony and often dreamed about the things they could do together. In one of his dreams, Jody was a ringmaster at a circus, putting his pony through its act.

Listen to the music Copland wrote for Jody's imaginary day at the circus.

"Circus Music" from
The Red Pony
.............Aaron Copland

CD 3-28

Listening for the Theme

Here is a melody, or theme, that Copland used in his "Circus Music."
Do you hear the theme in section A or in section B?

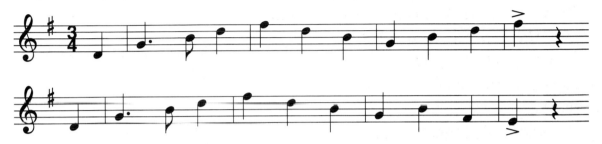

MEET THE COMPOSER

Aaron Copland (1900–1990)

Although Aaron Copland grew up in Brooklyn, New York, people often think of him as a westerner because of some of the music he composed. In pieces such as *Billy the Kid* and *Rodeo*, Copland used American cowboy songs and old fiddle tunes. In fact, Copland described himself as a "cowboy from Brooklyn."

In addition to *The Red Pony*, Copland wrote music for several other movies. He composed music for the stage and concert hall as well. Aaron Copland was one of America's finest composers. His music is heard and loved by audiences all over the world.

A ROUND FROM AFRICA

Can you sing "A Ram Sam Sam"? How will you create harmony for the song? Look for clues on the page.

A Ram Sam Sam   CD 3-29

Folk Song from Morocco

I   F

A ram sam sam, a ram sam sam,

C₇   F

Gu - li gu - li gu - li gu - li gu - li ram sam sam.

II   F

A ra - fi, a ra - fi,

C₇   F

Gu - li gu - li gu - li gu - li gu - li ram sam sam.

Tips for Singing

Singing well takes lots of energy and concentration. Here are some tips to help you sing your best.

- **Posture**

  Sit up straight, with your feet flat on the floor.

  OR

  Stand tall with your back straight. Keep your feet slightly apart, with one foot a little ahead of the other.

  Pretend that you have a string that comes out of the top of your head and connects you to the ceiling.

- **Breathing**

  Practice good breath control. When you inhale, keep your shoulders relaxed. Try to fill your rib cage with air.

  When you take a breath, make believe you are sipping air very quietly through a straw. As you exhale, pretend to cool a bowl of hot soup.

Practice these tips. Then try singing "A Ram Sam Sam" again. Can you sing each phrase on one breath? Can you sing two phrases on one breath?

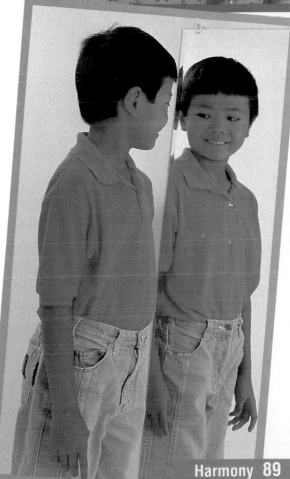

Two Melodies Together

Sometimes people make up a separate melody, or **countermelody**, to add harmony to a song. Listen for the melody and countermelody together in "Roll on the Ground."

Countermelody

Roll on, roll on, Roll, roll on, roll.

Roll on the Ground

Folk Song from Mississippi   **CD 3-30**

REFRAIN

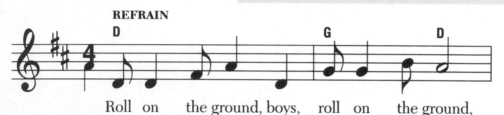

Roll on the ground, boys, roll on the ground,

Roll on the ground, boys, roll on the ground.

VERSE

1. Work on the rail - road, sleep on the ground,
2. Work on the rail - road, work all the day,

Eat so - dy crack - ers, and the wind blow them a - round.
Eat so - dy crack - ers, and the wind blow them a - way.

Transcribed and Adapted from the Library of Congress Field Recordings AFS 2594.

Add a Part

Here are two more melodies that can be played with "Roll on the Ground." Can you play them on the recorder or the bells?

Add a Countermelody

Listen to the recording of "Sweet Potatoes." Sing along when you can.

Sweet Potatoes   CD 3-31

Creole Folk Song

1. Soon as we all cook sweet po - ta - toes,
2. Soon as sup - per's done, Ma - ma hol - lers,

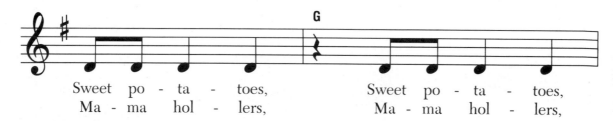

Sweet po - ta - toes,   Sweet po - ta - toes,
Ma - ma hol - lers,   Ma - ma hol - lers,

Soon as we all cook sweet po - ta - toes,
Soon as sup - per's done, Ma - ma hol - lers,

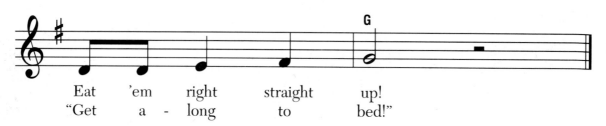

Eat 'em right straight up!
"Get a - long to bed!"

3. Soon's we touch our heads to the pillow, . . .
   Go to sleep right smart!

4. Soon's the rooster crow in the mornin', . . .
   Gotta wash our face!

When you know "Sweet Potatoes" well, learn to sing the countermelody, too.
Then your class can try singing the song and the countermelody together.

Roo, roo, roo, roo, hoo, hoo, Sing ho - ke dink-un!

Roo, roo, roo, roo, hoo, hoo, hoo, hoo!

Countermelodies to Play and Sing

Listen to "Hey, Dum Diddeley Dum." When you can sing the song, add harmony parts.

Hey, Dum Diddeley Dum

Words and Music by Marc Stone   CD 4-1

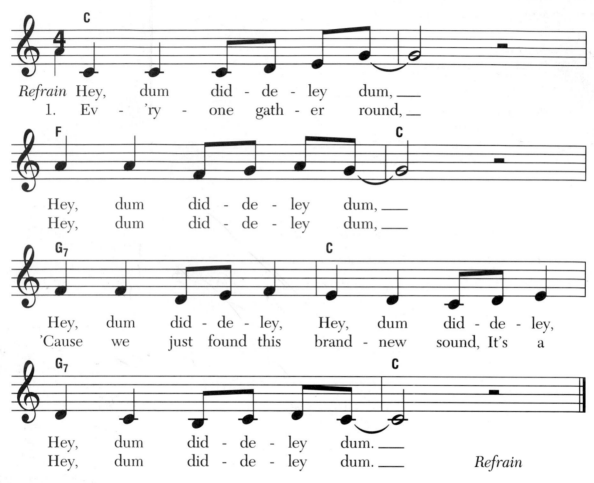

Refrain Hey,   dum   did - de - ley   dum, ___
1.   Ev - 'ry - one   gath - er   round, __

Hey,   dum   did - de - ley   dum, ___
Hey,   dum   did - de - ley   dum, ___

Hey,   dum   did - de - ley,   Hey,   dum   did - de - ley,
'Cause   we   just found this   brand - new   sound, It's   a

Hey,   dum   did - de - ley   dum. ___
Hey,   dum   did - de - ley   dum. ___   *Refrain*

2. Come and join in the fun,
    Hey, dum diddeley dum,
    We're gonna sing till the day is done,
    Hey, dum diddeley dum. *Refrain*

3. Ev'ryone come and sing,
    Hey, dum diddeley dum,
    We're gonna make these old rafters ring,
    Hey, dum diddeley dum. *Refrain*

Add Harmony Parts

In which direction do the tones move in this harmony part?

Play this part on bells or mallet instruments to accompany the song.

Here is another part to sing with "Hey, Dum Diddeley Dum."

Countermelody

Hey, dum did-de-ley dum, _

Hey, dum did-de-ley dum, _

Hey, dum did-de-ley, Hey, dum did-de-ley,

Hey, dum did-de-ley dum. _

Listen for the countermelodies in this recording.

Music Goes with Anything
..........Sarah Sterling and Robert Sterling

CD 4-2

A STORY IN MUSIC

Maurice Ravel composed a group of pieces called *Mother Goose Suite*, which tells the story of some favorite fairy tales. We know that music cannot tell a story as words do or paint a picture in lines and colors. Music can only suggest—make us think of a story or picture.

What does this music suggest to you?

CD 4-3 "The Conversations of Beauty and the Beast" from *Mother Goose Suite*.............Maurice Ravel

The Conversation

At the beginning of the piece, you hear Beauty's voice.

Then the Beast speaks.

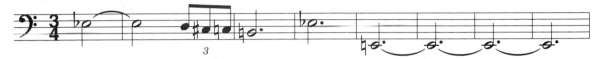

Can you hear the place in the music where Beauty and the Beast talk at the same time?

MEET THE COMPOSER

Maurice Ravel was born in southwestern France in 1875. Maurice learned to play the piano when he was still a child. As he grew older, he became fascinated with the instruments of the orchestra. He wanted to know how each instrument worked—how it sounded, how high and low it could play. Ravel was also interested in composing, and before he was 20 years old, he began writing music of his own.

Mother Goose Suite was first written for piano. Later on, when Ravel rewrote the piece for orchestra, he was careful to choose the instrument that would best suit each character in his musical story.

Maurice Ravel (1875–1937)

Colorful Sounds

The composer of this song was not thinking of colors like blue and red. Can you guess what he means by *the color of music*?

The Color of Music   CD 4-4, 5

Words and Music by David Eddleman

1. What col - or is the sound of a vi - o - lin?

What col - or is the sound of a lute?

What col - or is the sound of the room you're in

when there's some - one there who's play - ing a flute?

What col - ors are the fife and the drum

© 1991 David Eddleman

when they come march - ing through the square?

They're the col-or of mu - sic paint-ed in the air. _____

2. What color do you hear when a singer sings?
   What color is a trumpet blare?
   What color do you hear when a church bell rings,
      when the timpani are drummed in a pair?
   What color is the mellow sound of a cello
      when a bow runs across the strings?
   It's the color of music and, oh, what a joy it brings.

3. What color do you hear when the oboe calls?
   What color do you hear in the horn?
   What color do you hear in a concert hall
      when the notes are just being born?
   The bassoon that croons its lovely tunes
      is a color that's rich and round.
   It's the color of music in a rainbow world
      of sound.(2 times)

The Sound of Voices

No other person in the world has a voice that sounds exactly like yours. Each voice is different. When friends and family call you on the telephone, you know who is calling before being told. You know this by the special sound of each voice.

Follow the words of the poem "The Wind" as you listen to the recording. Do you hear one voice? Several voices?

The Wind CD 4-6

I saw you toss the kites on high
And blow the birds about the sky;
And all around I heard you pass,
Like ladies' skirts across the grass—
     O wind, a-blowing all day long,
     O wind, that sings so loud a song!

I saw the different things you did,
But always you yourself you hid.
I felt you push, I heard you call,
I could not see yourself at all—
     O wind, a-blowing all day long,
     O wind, that sings so loud a song!

O you that are so strong and cold,
O blower, are you young or old?
Are you a beast of field and tree,
Or just a stronger child than me?
     O wind, a-blowing all day long,
     O wind, that sings so loud a song!

—Robert Louis Stevenson

What words in the poem "Weather"
remind you of the sound of rain?

How can you use your voice to "paint"
the sounds in this poem? Try reading it
aloud for your classmates.

Weather

Dot a dot dot dot a dot dot
Spotting the windowpane.
Spack a spack speck flick a flack fleck
Freckling the windowpane.

A spatter a scatter a wet cat a clatter
A splatter a rumble outside.
Umbrella umbrella umbrella umbrella
Bumbershoot barrel of rain.

Slosh a galosh slosh a galosh
Slithor and slather a glide
A puddle a jump a puddle a jump
A puddle a pump aluddle a dump a
Puddmuddle jump in and slide!

—Eve Merriam

A MUSICAL

The African American spiritual is a musical form that uses **call-and-response** singing. In many spirituals, one singer may have a part to perform all alone. The part is called a **solo**.

As you listen to "Oh, Won't You Sit Down?" notice how the chorus answers the soloists. Together they create a musical conversation.

Oh, Won't You Sit Down? CD 4-7

African American Spiritual

A REFRAIN
Solo — G — Chorus — D₇

Oh, won't you sit down? __ Lord, I can't sit down.

Solo — G — Chorus — D₇

Oh, won't you sit down? __ Lord, I can't sit down.

Solo — G — Chorus — D₇

Oh, won't you sit down? __ Lord, I can't sit down.

G — D₇ — G — Fine

'Cause I just got to Heav-en, gon-na look a-round. __

CONVERSATION

Listen for the call-and-response
singing in these two selections.

CD 4-8 *Ain't That Love*
...............Ray Charles

CD 4-9 *Lifikile Evangeli*
............Ladysmith Black Mambazo

B **VERSE**
Solo
G

1. Who's that yon - der dressed in red? ___

Chorus
G   D₇   G

Must be the chil - dren that ___ Mo - ses led. ___

Solo
G

Who's that yon - der dressed in white? ___

Chorus
G   D₇   *D.C. al Fine*
                                                     G

Must be the chil - dren of the Is - rael - ite. ___

2. Who's that yonder dressed in blue?
   Must be the children that are comin' through.
   Who's that yonder dressed in black?
   Must be the hypocrites a-turnin' back. *Refrain*

Fare thee well, __ fare thee well, __ Fare thee well my fair - y fay, __

For I'm goin' to Loui - si - an - a, For to see my Su - sy - an - na,

Sing-ing Pol - ly Wol - ly Doo-dle all the day. __

3. The partridge is a pretty bird,
   It has a speckled breast;
   It steals away the farmer's grain,
   And totes it to its nest! *Refrain*

4. The raccoon's tailed is ringed around,
   The 'possum's tail is bare;
   The rabbit's got no tail at all,
   Just a little bitty bunch of hair! *Refrain*

PERCUSSION INSTRUMENTS

Percussion instruments are instruments that are struck, scraped, or shaken. They are probably the oldest known instruments.

Listen to this piece for percussion instruments. Do you hear any instruments that you know?

Pulse (excerpt)
..........................Henry Cowell

CD 4-12

The String Quartet

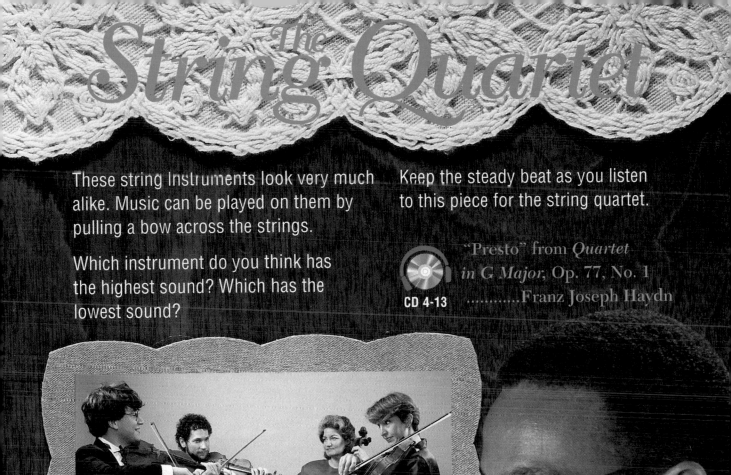

These string instruments look very much alike. Music can be played on them by pulling a bow across the strings.

Which instrument do you think has the highest sound? Which has the lowest sound?

Keep the steady beat as you listen to this piece for the string quartet.

"Presto" from *Quartet in G Major*, Op. 77, No. 1 ....Franz Joseph Haydn

CD 4-13

The Woodwind Quintet

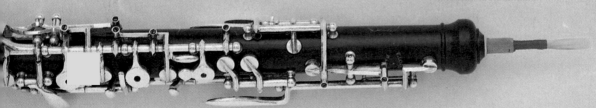

Which of the instruments in the photograph is not a woodwind?

Which one do you think has the highest sound? The lowest?

Listen to this piece for woodwind quintet. What words would you use to describe the music?

Scherzo .... Eugène Bozza

CD 4-14

BRASS INSTRUMENTS

These are the brass instruments found in most orchestras and bands. Which one do you think has the highest sound? The lowest?

Brass instruments are used for announcing important events. They also play in parades. Do you know why?

Listen to this piece for five brass instruments. How many times do you hear the first melody?

Rondeau
............Jean-Joseph Mouret

CD 4-15

winds around the world

People have been playing wind instruments for thousands of years. Wind instruments are made of wood, bamboo, and metal. Today we also make them out of plastic. Wind instruments are played all over the world.

The shakuhachi comes from Japan. It is made of bamboo and sounds like a human singing voice. The player can also produce unusual airy sounds on the instrument.

Mountains Before Snow (excerpt)
..............Traditional Song
from Japan

CD 4-16

You may think of Scotland when you hear a bagpipe, but bagpipes are played in many different countries. The player blows air into the bag. The player's arm then squeezes the bag and pushes the air through reeds inside the instrument.

Regimental March ....Traditional Song from Scotland

CD 4-17

Panpipes are a set of flutes of different lengths that are tied together. Each pipe plays only one pitch. To change pitch, a player blows across the top holes while moving the instrument. Panpipes are played in many countries and are very important in Peru and Bolivia.

CD 4-18

THEMES

Where do you hear music each day?

On the radio? On television?
At school concerts?
On the playground singing songs
with your friends?

This section connects you
with many different kinds of people and
the many ways we all use music.

You will sing songs about living
and working together with your neighbors.
You will hear music from the United States and
from around the world. You will learn
silly songs that stretch your imagination and
serious songs about freedom for all people.
And you can put on a musical
production with your class!

Music can connect you with all kinds of
people-people just like you and people
different from you!

section 2

CARING FOR

Each of us is responsible for our world.
What can you do to help save the planet?

Save the Planet
CD 4-20, 21

Words by Gene Grier   Music by Gene Grier and Lowell Everson

A REFRAIN

Save   the   plan – et   and ev-'ry-thing on ___ it.

We've got   to   do ___ it   to - day. ___

Last time
to Coda

Save   the   plan – et   and ev-'ry-thing on ___ it.

1.,3.   *To verse*   2.

We've got   to   start ___ right a - way! ___   ___

B VERSE

There are   some prob-lems for   you ___   and me ___

THE EARTH

Listen to this Russian folk song about the beauty of our earth.

Garden of the Earth
..........Folk Song from Russia
(Paul Winter and Paul Halley)

CD 4-22

to solve with-out ___ de - lay. ___

We'll set ex - am - ples for all ___ to see ___

D.C.

and we will show ___ the way. ___

Coda

We've got to start, all do our part,

we've got to start ___ right a - way! ___

Sing About Your Land

Woody Guthrie was a folk singer who made up hundreds of songs about the United States. This is probably his best-known song.

If you made up a song about your land, what are some of the things you might include in your song?

This Land Is Your Land

CD 4-23

Words and Music by Woody Guthrie

REFRAIN

This land is your land, ___ This land is my land ___

From Cal - i - for - nia ___ to the New York is - land; ___

From the red-wood for - est ___ to the Gulf Stream wa - ters; ___

This land was made for you and me. ___

VERSE

1. As I was walk - ing ___ that rib-bon of high - way, ___

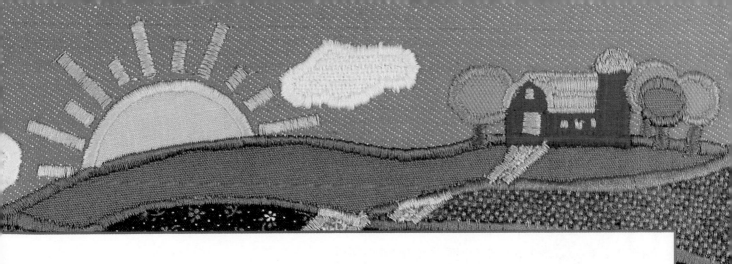

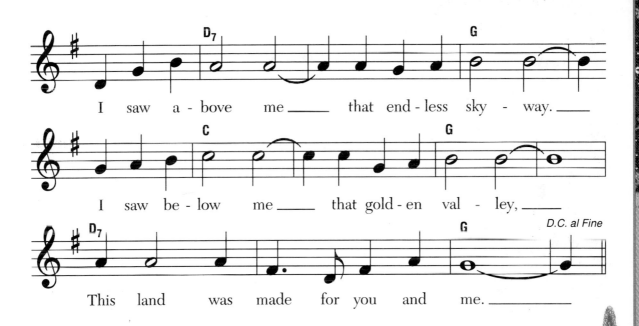

I saw a-bove me ____ that end-less sky - way. ____

I saw be-low me ____ that gold-en val - ley, ____

D.C. al Fine

This land was made for you and me. _____

2. I've roamed and rambled and I followed my footsteps
To the sparkling sands of her diamond deserts,
And all around me a voice was sounding,
"This land was made for you and me." *Refrain*

3. When the sun comes shining and I was strolling
And the wheatfields waving and the dust clouds rolling,
As the fog was lifting, a voice was chanting,
"This land was made for you and me." *Refrain*

We can all do things to make our world brighter, and a good place to start is in our own backyards. Listen to this song about growing a garden. What kinds of things could you grow in a garden?

Garden Song   CD 4-24

Words and Music by David Mallett

1. Inch by inch, row by row, ___
2. Pull - in' weeds and pick - in' stones, _

Gon - na make this gar - den grow, ___
Man is made of dreams and bones, _

All it takes is a rake and a hoe
Feel the need to ___ grow my ___ own

and a piece of fer - tile ground. _
'cause the time is close at hand. ___

Inch by inch, row by row, —
Grain for grain, sun and rain, —

Some - one bless the seeds I sow,
Find my way in na - ture's chain,

Some-one warm them from be - low —
Tune my bod - y and my brain

'til the rain comes tum - bl - ing down.
to the mu - sic from — the land.

3. Plant your rows straight and strong,
Temper them with prayer and song,
Mother Earth will make you strong
if you give her love and care.
Old crow watching hungrily
From his perch in yonder tree,
In my garden I'm as free
as that feathered thief up there.

A Thing of Beauty

You may not see things exactly the same way that others do. What do you think is meant by the phrase *beauty lies in the eye of the beholder*?

Everything Is Beautiful CD 4-25, 26

Words and Music by Ray Stevens

A *With a swing*

Ev-'ry-thing is beau - ti - ful   in its own   way, ___

like a star-ry sum-mer night or a snow-cov-ered win-ter's _ day.

Ev-'ry-bod-y's beau - ti - ful   in their own   way, ___

Fine

un-der God's heav - en   the world's gon-na find _ a __ way.

B

There is none so   blind _   as   one who will not   see. ___

We must not close our minds. _ We must let our thoughts be free. _

For ev - 'ry hour that pass - es by, ____

you know the world gets a lit - tle bit old - er.

It's time to re - a - lize that beau - ty lies

D.C. al Fine

in the eye ____ of the be - hold - er. _____

Walk, Talk, Sing, and Shout

Walk Together, Children

African American Spiritual   CD 4-27, 28

What do you think the words of this African American spiritual mean? How would you describe the mood of this song?

1. Oh, walk to-geth-er, chil-dren,   Don't you get __ wea - ry,
2. Oh, talk to-geth-er, chil-dren,   Don't you get __ wea - ry,

Walk to-geth-er, chil-dren,   Don't you get   wea - ry,
Talk to-geth-er, chil-dren,   Don't you get   wea - ry,

Oh, walk to-geth-er, chil-dren,   Don't you get __ wea - ry,
Oh, talk to-geth-er, chil-dren,   Don't you get __ wea - ry,

There's a great camp - meet-ing in the prom-ised land.
There's a great camp - meet-ing in the prom-ised land.

3. Oh, sing together, children, . . .

4. Oh, shout together, children, . . .

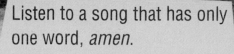

Listen to a song that has only one word, *amen*.

CD 4-29

Amen..............
African American
Spiritual

West Church, Boston   *Maurice Brazil Prendergast*

Hayden Collection Charles Henry Hayden Fund. Courtesy, Museum of Fine Arts, Boston.

A Musical Greeting

Why would this be a good song to sing for United Nations Day?

We Come to Greet You in Peace CD 5-1
(Hevenu Shalom Aleichem)

Hebrew Folk Song

We come to greet you in peace, __ We come to
He - ve - nu sha - lom a - lei - chem, He - ve - nu

greet you in peace, __ We come to greet __ you in
sha - lom a - lei - chem, He - ve - nu sha - lom a -

peace, __ We come to greet you, greet you,
lei - chem, He - ve - nu sha - lom, sha - lom,

1. greet __ you in peace. We come to
sha - lom a - lei - chem. He - ve - nu

2. greet __ you in peace.
sha - lom a - lei - chem.

Play this tambourine accompaniment throughout the song.

This poem was written by a nine-year-old girl from California. Listen as she reads her poem about peace.

The Peace Dove CD 5-2

A dove flies with the soft wind
And swoops down under the fog,
Drifting above the deep blue ocean.
She is the peace dove.

When I look at her,
I can feel her soft glow
Reflecting off her fluorescent white feathers.
She fills me with respect for Mother Earth.
She is the peace dove.

I feel her gentle presence.
It is a peaceful, loving feeling,
Almost like nothing is there
But me, and her,
And the roar of the wondrous ocean.
She is the peace dove.

—Oceanna Chatard

A Garden of People

This song is about a special garden. What four things named in this song help the garden grow?

Each of Us Is a Flower

Words and Music by Charlotte Diamond   **CD 5-3**

Each of us ___ is a flow - er,

Grow-ing in ___ life's ___ gar - den. ___

Each of us ___ is a flow - er,

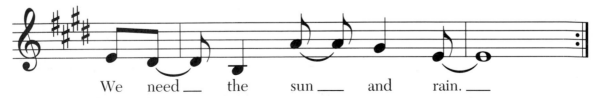

We need ___ the sun ___ and rain. ___

B

Sun, _____ shine your warmth on ___ me.

Moon, _____ cool me with your _ night.

Wind, _____ bring the gen - tle ___ rain.

Earth, _____ dig my roots down deep.

All Different

Make a Rainbow

CD 5-4, 5

Words and Music by Portia Nelson

It takes many colors to create a rainbow

Red and white and black and ___ yel - low,
Or - ange ice and mead - ows of mar - i - gold,

Tan and brown and tear - ful blue;
Pink bal - loons and ted - dy - bear brown;

These are the col - ors of chil - dren ev - 'ry - where;
These are the col - ors that chil - dren ev - 'ry - where

1. Just like me and you.
2. Love to have a - round.

Make a rain-bow, Make a rain-bow, Let the col-ors dance and shine.

Make a rain - bow till that rain - bow is a beau-ti - ful de-sign

Colors!

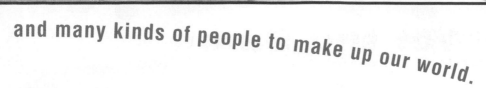

and many kinds of people to make up our world.

Of red and white and black and ___ yel - low,

All so dif - f'rent, yet the same.

Rain-bows will spar-kle when chil-dren ev-'ry-where an-swer to one name.

Make a rain-bow, Make a rain-bow till the skies are clear a-bove;

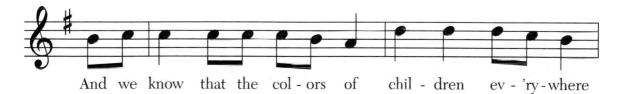

And we know that the col-ors of chil - dren ev - 'ry-where

Shine in a world of love.

DIFFERENT
Yet the Same

Americans are as different as can be. Our country is made up of people from many places in the world. This song tells of folks who are different, yet hope for the same thing—peace.

How are you different from your best friend?
How are you the same?

American Children CD 5-6, 7

Words and Music by Marc Black and Ed Bialek

VERSE

1. Some folks like clas - si - cal, Some folks like rock 'n' roll.

Some folks like reg - gae, and dance all day long.

Some folks fight fires, __ and some folks change tires. __

Some folks fix ra - di - os, We all hope for peace.

REFRAIN

We are ___ all ___ A - mer - i - can chil - dren,

All of us dif-f'rent, We all hope for peace.

2. Jamie likes soccer,
   And Frankie shoots hoops.
   Sarah plays hockey,
   She's the best on the team.
   My best friend lives in Baltimore.
   Uncle Mitch is in Kansas.
   Aunt Jane lives in Santa Fe.
   We all hope for peace. *Refrain*

Each state has its favorite songs. What can you learn about Texas by reading the words of this song?

Follow the music as you listen to the song. Can you find three more places where the tones repeat just as they do in the color box?

Deep in the Heart of Texas

CD 5-8

Words by June Hershey   Music by Don Swander

The stars at night are big and bright,

Deep in the heart of Tex - as; ____

The prai - rie sky is wide and high,

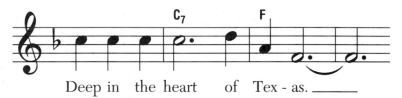

Deep in the heart of Tex - as. ____

A LONE STAR STATE FAVORITE

Play the repeated tones every time they appear in the song.

Mallet instrument or Recorder

C

F

The sage in bloom is like per-fume,

Deep in the heart of Tex-as; _____

Re-minds me of the one I love,

Deep in the heart of Tex-as. _____

This listening piece comes from a ballet called *Rodeo*. The story of *Rodeo* is set on a ranch in Texas.

CD 5-9

"Hoe-Down" from *Rodeo* ....Aaron Copland

Mother Corn

The Native Americans taught the early settlers how to raise corn.

The Pawnee Indians spoke of corn as *Atira*, meaning "mother." *H* means "breath of life." You can see how important corn was in their lives. They sang this song to celebrate the harvest.

H'Atira   CD 5-10

Pawnee Corn Song

Fol-low Moth-er Corn, Who breathes forth life.

H'A - ti - ra,   H'A - ti - ra,   H'A - ti - ra,   A - ti - ra,

H'A - ti - ra,   A - ti - ra,   H'A - ti - ra,   A - ti - ra,

A - ti - ra,   H'A - ti - ra,   A - ti - ra.

Drum and Rattle

Play the drum and rattle patterns as an introduction.
You can also use the patterns to accompany the song.

Drum

Rattle

Nicely, Nicely

Nicely, nicely, nicely, away in the east,
the rain clouds care for the little corn plants
as a mother cares for her baby.

—*From a Zuni Corn Ceremony*

Mother Corn   *Pawnee*

Music from the

Daybreak Vision was composed and performed by R. Carlos Nakai, a Native American of Navajo and Ute heritage. Nakai began performing in the 1970s, when he was given a flute as a gift. His concerts and recordings include traditional Navajo and Ute music as well as his own new compositions.

What kind of instrument do you hear in this recording? What kind of picture do you see in your mind when you hear this music?

Daybreak Vision
by R. Carlos Nakai

CD 5-11

R. Carlos Nakai

First Americans

Bear Dance Song comes from the Southern Ute tribe of Colorado. The dance is performed every spring, when the bear awakens from its hibernation. *Bear Dance Song* is performed on this recording by the American Indian Dance Theater.

Listen for the sound of the bear in this music. It is produced by an instrument called a bear growler. You can find a picture of one on p. 304.

CD 5-12

Bear Dance Song
Southern Ute
Dance Song

American Indian Dance Theater

Native American Instruments

Drum

Rattle

Music is a part of Native American culture. The songs and dances are sometimes accompanied by instruments. The materials for making these instruments are found in nature.

Drums are important to Native American music. The drum above can be played on either side.

The rattle is another popular instrument. It can be made in many different ways. This one is made by hanging deer hoofs on a stick.

Rattle

Another way a rattle can be made is to let the seeds in a gourd dry. When you shake it, you can hear the seeds moving.

Rasp

This musical rasp is made by carving notches in a piece of wood. The player runs a scraper over the notches.

Flute

The most common Native American melody instrument is the flute. This one is made from wood.

A MEXICAN

> "De colores" tells about the great beauty that can be found in the colors of nature.

De colores　CD 5-13

English Words by Alice Firgau　Folk Song from Mexico

De _____ co - lo - res, ___ De co - lo - res se vis - ten
When ___ the mead - ows, ___ when the mead-ows burst forth in

los cam - pos en la pri - ma - ve - ra, _____
the cool dew - y col - ors of spring-time; _____

De _____ co - lo - res, ___ De co - lo - res son los pa - ja - ri - tos
When ___ the swal - lows, __ when the swal-lows come wing-ing in clouds of

que vie - nen de a - fue - ra, _____
bright col - ors from far - off; _____

De _____ co - lo - res, _____
When _____ the rain - bow, _____

AMERICAN FAVORITE

De co - lo - res es el ar - co i - ris
when the rain - bow spreads rib - bons of col - or

que ve - mos lu - cir, _____
all o - ver the sky: _____

y por e - so los gran - des a - mo - res
Then I know why the splen - dors of true love

de mu - chos co - lo - res me gus - tan a mí. _____
are great and their col - ors, the best ones of all. _____

gus - tan a mí. _____
best ones of all. _____

Sing a Spiritual

When singing African American spirituals, performers sometimes make up new verses. You, too, can make up new verses to sing with this melody. Teach your classmates to sing your new verse.

He's Got the Whole World in His Hands   CD 5-14

African American Spiritual

1. He's got the whole world — in his hands, ___
   He's got the whole world — in his hands, ___

He's got the whole world — in his hands, ___

He's got the whole world in his hands. _____

2. He's got the wind and rain in his hands, *(3 times)*
   He's got the whole world in his hands.

3. He's got-a you and me, brother, in his hands,
   He's got-a you and me, sister, in his hands,
   He's got-a you and me, brother, in his hands,
   He's got the whole world in his hands.

Look at the music in the color box. Can you find another phrase that looks exactly like it?

Try playing the two phrases on the keyboard.

LOOK AWAY

The African American spiritual is a religious folk song that often speaks of hope for a happier life.

"Do, Lord" has two sections, a refrain and a verse. Which section is repeated?

The Creation of the Animals   *Harriet Powers*

Do, Lord   CD 5-17, 18

African American Spiritual

REFRAIN

Do, Lord,   oh   do, Lord,   oh   do   re-mem-ber   me,

Do, Lord,   oh   do, Lord,   oh   do   re-mem-ber   me.

Do,   Lord,   oh   do,   Lord,   oh   do   re-mem-ber   me,

Look   a-way   be-yond___   the   blue.

Here is a recorder part for "Do, Lord" that uses only three notes.
Can you can play it while your class sings the song?

VERSE

I got a home in glo - ry land that out-shines the sun,

I got a home in glo - ry land that out-shines the sun.

I got a home in glo - ry land that out - shines the sun,

D.C. al Fine

Look a - way be - yond the blue.

The American cowboy often made his home outdoors. In this song, a cowboy sings of the beauty of that home.

A Home

Home on the Range CD 5-19

Cowboy Song from the United States

1. Oh, give me a home where the buf - fa - lo roam,
2. How of - ten at night when the heav - ens are bright

Where the deer and the an - te - lope play, _____
With the lights from the glit - ter - ing stars, _____

Where sel - dom is heard a dis - cour - ag - ing word,
Have I stood there a - mazed and _ asked as I gazed,

And the skies are not cloud - y all day. _____
If their glo - ry ex - ceeds that of ours. _____

Under the Stars

REFRAIN

Home, home on the range, _____

Where the deer and the an - te - lope play, _____

Where sel - dom is heard a dis - cour - ag - ing word,

And the skies are not cloud - y all day. _____

Way Out WEST

This is a song that was sung by someone who went out west to become a cowhand. Although the work was hard, he decided to settle down in Montana.

My Home's in Montana

CD 5-20

Words Adapted by W. S. Williams   *Cowboy Song from the United States*

1. My home's in Mon-tan-a, I left In-di-an-a
2. I learned how to las-so way down in El Pa-so,

To start a new life far a-way in the West;
I've fol-lowed the cat-tle wher-ev-er they roam;

My skin's rough as leath-er, made tough by the weath-er;
I'm wear-y of stray-ing, right here I'll be stay-ing,

The wind and the sun of the land I love best.
I'll wan-der no more for Mon-tan-a's my home.

Play a Part

Choose one of these patterns to accompany "My Home's in Montana."
Which pattern will you choose? Play it all through the song.

1.
2.
3.
4.

Cowboy Singing   *Thomas Eakins*

A Yankee Doodle

Beat

"Yankee Doodle" is a favorite song of boys and girls all over America. Many verses have been written for the tune. Here are the words that you may know best.

Yankee Doodle came to town
Riding on a pony,
Stuck a feather in his cap
And called it macaroni.

Yankee Doodle   CD 5-21

Words by Dr. Richard Shuckburgh   *Traditional*

1. ⸲ Fath'r and I went down to camp,
2. And there we saw a thou-sand men,

A - long with Cap - tain Good - in',
As rich as Squire __ Da - vid;

And there we saw the men and boys
And what they wast - ed ev - 'ry day,

Parts for Percussion

Which percussion part will you play? Which instrument will you use to accompany this marching song?

As thick as hast - y pud - din'.
I wish it could be sav - ed.

REFRAIN

Yan - kee Doo - dle, keep it up, Yan - kee Doo - dle dan - dy,

Mind the mu - sic and the step And with the girls be hand - y.

3. And there was Captain Washington
Upon a slapping stallion,
A-giving orders to his men;
I guess there was a million. *Refrain*

Imagine That!

The lady in this song has a strange diet. Listen for the surprise ending.

Copyright © 1950 and 1960 by Peer International (Canada) Ltd. Sole Selling Agent Peer International Corporation. Used by permission.

Listen to the King's Singers' version of this song. What do they do with their voices to make the song fun and interesting?

CD 5-24

I Know an Old Woman
..........Rose Bonne
and Alan Mills

B♭ **G₇** **C** **C₇**

who swal-lowed a
bird!	Now, how	ab - surd,	to swal - low	a	bird!
cat!	Now, fan - cy	that,	to swal - low	a	cat!
dog!	My, what	a hog,	to swal - low	a	dog!
goat!	Just opened her	throat	and swal-lowed	a	goat!
cow!	I don't know	how	she swal-lowed	a	cow!

F

No repeat first time

3. She swal-lowed the bird to catch the spi - der
4. She swal-lowed the cat to catch the bird, ___ *(To 3)*
5. She swal-lowed the dog to catch the cat, ___ *(To 4)*
6. She swal-lowed the goat to catch the dog, ___ *(To 5)*
7. She swal-lowed the cow to catch the goat, ___ *(To 6)*

C **G₇** **C** **C₇** *D.S.*

that wrig - gled and wrig - gled and tick - led in - side her,

Coda **F** *(Spoken)*

8. I know an old la - dy who swal-lowed a horse; She's dead, of course!

Never Smile at a Crocodile

from *Peter Pan*   CD 5-25, 26

Words by Jack Lawrence   Music by Frank Churchill

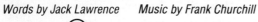

Nev - er   smile   at   a   croc - o - dile,

No,   you   can't   get   friend - ly   with   a   croc - o - dile,

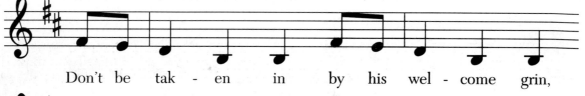

Don't   be   tak - en   in   by   his   wel - come   grin,

He's im - ag - in - ing how well you'd fit with - in   his   skin.

Nev - er   smile   at   a   croc - o - dile,

How Doth the Little Crocodile

How doth the little crocodile
  Improve his shining tail,
And pour the waters of the Nile
  On every golden scale!

How cheerfully he seems to grin,
  How neatly spreads his claws,
And welcomes little fishes in,
  With gently smiling jaws!

—Lewis Carroll

Nev - er   tip   your   hat   and   stop   to   talk   a   while.

1.,2. Nev - er   run,   walk a - way,   say "Good-night," not "Good day!"
   3. Don't be   rude,   nev - er mock, throw a   kiss,   not   a   rock.

Clear the aisle and nev - er smile at Mis - ter Croc - o - dile.

B

You may ve - ry well be well-bred, Lots of   et - i - quette in your head,

But   there's   al - ways   some   spe - cial   case,

D.C. al Fine

time   or   place   to   for - get   et - i - quette.

A Fantasy Land

Many people who moved to the United States from other countries came here to start a better life. The farmers from Norway thought Oleana would be a good place to settle. Do you think they *really* believed the words of this song?

Oleana CD 5-27

English Words by Polly Budd　　Emigrant Song from Norway

1. O - le-an - a, O - le - an - a, Far a - cross the deep blue sea,

REFRAIN: O - le, O - le - an - a, ____ O - le, O - le - an - a,

O - le - an - a, O - le - an - a, That is where I'd like to be.

O - le, O - le, O - le, O - le, O - le, O - le - an - a.

2. Oleana, that's the place,
   That is where I'll settle down;
   It's a place where land is free
   And money trees grow all around.
   Refrain

3. Corn and wheat grow to the sky,
   All according to the plan;
   Sheep and cows do all the work
   And fish jump in the frying pan.
   Refrain

4. There the crops just plant themselves,
   There the sun shines night and day;
   Harvest time comes once a month,
   But farmers only sing and play.
   Refrain

5. Ole Bull will play for us,
   Play upon his violin;
   And we'll sing and dance together,
   Happier than we've ever been.
   Refrain

Patterns to Play

Try playing these ostinatos on mallet instruments.

Then add a tambourine part.

What Do You Wish For?

Each of the characters in this song is wishing for something. Listen to find out who they are and what each one is looking for.

If I Only Had a Brain
from *The Wizard of Oz*   CD 5-28, 29

Words by E. Y. Harburg   Music by Harold Arlen

(*Scarecrow*) 1. I could while a-way the hours __ con-fer-rin' with the flow-ers,
I'd un-rav-el ev-'ry rid-dle for an-y in-di-vid-le
I would not be just a nuff-in', my head all full of stuff-in',

con - sult - in' with the rain;
in trou - ble or in pain;
my heart all full of pain;

And my head, I'd be scratch-in' while my thoughts were bus-y hatch-in',
With the thoughts I'd be think-in', I could be an-oth-er Lin-coln,
And per-haps I'd de-serve you and be ev-en wor-thy erv you,

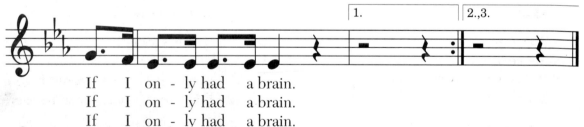

1.   2.,3.

If I on - ly had a brain.
If I on - ly had a brain.
If I on - ly had a brain.

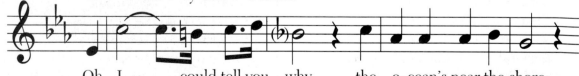

Oh, I _____ could tell you why the o-cean's near the shore;

I could think of things I nev - er thunk be - fore,

and then I'd sit and think some more.

D.C.

(Tin Woodman)

2. When a man's an empty kettle,
   he should be on his mettle,
   and yet I'm torn apart;
   Just because I'm presumin'
   that I could be kinda human,
   If I only had a heart.

   I'd be tender, I'd be gentle,
   and awful sentimental
   regarding love and art;
   I'd be friends with the sparrows
   and the boy that shoots the arrows,
   If I only had a heart.

   Picture me, a balcony,
   above a voice sings low,
   'Wherefore art thou, Romeo?'
   I hear a beat–and think "How sweet!"

   Just to register emotion,
   "Jealousy," "Devotion,"
   and really feel the part,
   I would stay young and chipper
   and I'd lock it with a zipper,
   If I only had a heart.

(Cowardly Lion)

3. Life is sad, believe me, missy,
   when you're born to be a sissy,
   without the vim and verve;
   But I could change my habits,
   never more be scared of rabbits,
   If I only had the nerve.

   I'm afraid there's no denyin'
   I'm just a dandylion,
   a fate I don't deserve;
   But I could show my prowess,
   be a lion, not a mowess,
   If I only had the nerve.

   Oh, I'd be in my stride,
   a king down to the core;
   Oh, I'd roar the way I never roared before,
   And then I'd *rrrwoof*, and roar some more.

   I would show the dinosaurus
   who's king around the fores',
   a king they'd better serve;
   Why, with my regal beezer
   I could be another Caesar,
   If I only had the nerve.

A Funny Story

A **ballad** is a song that tells a story. In this humorous ballad from Mexico, you will hear about the adventures of a cat named Señor Don Gato.

Don Gato CD 6-1, 2

English Words by Margaret Marks   *Folk Song from Mexico*

1. Oh, Se-ñor Don Ga - to was a cat,____
1. *El se - ñor don Ga - to_es - ta - ba____*

On a high, red roof Don Ga - to sat.____
sen - ta - di - to_en el te - ja - do____

He went there to read a let - ter, meow, meow, meow,
cuan - do le vi - nie - ron car - tas, mia - rra - miau,

Where the read - ing light was bet - ter, meow, meow, meow,
cuan - do le vi - nie - ron car - tas, mia - rra - miau,

'Twas a love note for Don Ga - to!____
si que - rí - a ser ca - sa - do.____

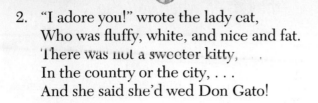

2. "I adore you!" wrote the lady cat,
Who was fluffy, white, and nice and fat.
There was not a sweeter kitty,
In the country or the city, . . .
And she said she'd wed Don Gato!

3. Oh, Don Gato jumped so happily,
He fell off the roof and broke his knee,
Broke his ribs and all his whiskers, . . .
And his little solar plexus, . . .
"¡Ay caramba!" cried Don Gato!

4. Then the doctors all came on the run
Just to see if something could be done,
And they held a consultation, . . .
About how to save their patient, . . .
How to save Señor Don Gato!

5. But in spite of ev'rything they tried,
Poor Señor Don Gato up and died,
Oh, it wasn't very merry,
Going to the cemetery, . . .
For the ending of Don Gato!

6. When the funeral passed the market square,
Such a smell of fish was in the air,
Though his burial was slated, . . .
He became re-animated! . . .
He came back to life, Don Gato!

2. Con una gatita blanca,
sobrina de un gato pardo,
que no la había más linda, . . .
que no la había más linda, . . .
en las casas de aquel barrio.

3. Don Gato con la alegría,
se ha caído del tejado;
ha roto siete costillas, . . .
ha roto siete costillas, . . .
las dos orejas y el rabo.

4. A visitarlo venían,
médicos y cirujanos;
todos dicen que se muere, . . .
todos dicen que se muere, . . .
que don Gato está muy malo.

5. El gatito ya se ha muerto,
ya se ha muerto el buen don Gato;
a enterrar ya se lo llevan, . . .
a enterrar ya se lo llevan, . . .
todos los gatos llorando.

6. Cuando pasaba el entierro,
por la plaza del pescado,
al olor de las sardinas, . . .
al olor de las sardinas, . . .
don Gato ha resucitado.

Listen to the verses of this song for the three ways Freddie Wilson tried to get rid of his cat. Sing along on the refrain when you can.

But the Cat Came Back CD 6-3

Words and Music by Josef Marais

1. Fred-die Wil-son had a cat that he did-n't want to keep.

He of-fered him for free and he tried to sell him cheap.

He called up-on the preach-er one Sun-day for ad-vice;

The preach-er said, "Yes, leave him here, it would be so nice!"

But the cat came back, he would-n't stay a-way,

He was sit - tin' on the porch on the ver - y next day.

The cat came back, he did - n't want to roam,

The ver - y next day it was "Home, Sweet Home."

2. Freddie put him on a ship and they headed for Ceylon.
   The ship was overloaded more than twenty thousand ton.
   Not far away from shore the cargo ship went down,
   There wasn't any doubt about it, everybody drowned.   *Refrain*

3. Then he put the cat aboard with a man in a balloon,
   Who would give the cat away to the man in the moon.
   The balloon it didn't rise, it burst in bits instead,
   And ten miles from the spot, they found the man stone dead.   *Refrain*

Talking with Tickle

Tune

Tickle Tune Typhoon is a singing group who performs especially for children and their families. Listen as members of Tickle Tune Typhoon talk about their work as musicians.

Careers in Music
..........Tickle Tune Typhoon

CD 6-4

C☼UNTING in SPANISH

This is how to count from one to seven in Spanish: *uno, dos, tres, cuatro, cinco, seis, siete.*

This is how to count the weeks in Spanish: *una semana, dos semanas, tres semanas, cuatro semanas, cinco semanas, seis semanas, siete semanas.*

The Tiny Boat (El barquito) CD 6-5

English Words by Kim Williams *Folk Song from Latin America*

Oh, there was once a boat so ve - ry ti - ny,
Ha - bía u - na vez un bar - co chi - qui - ti - co,

Oh, there was once a boat so ve - ry ti - ny,
Ha - bía u - na vez un bar - co chi - qui - ti - co,

Oh, there was once a boat so ve - ry ti - ny,
Ha - bía u - na vez un bar - co chi - qui - ti - co,

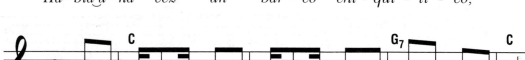

So ve - ry ti - ny, so ve - ry ti - ny, it could not e - ven sail a - way.
Que no po - dí - a, que no po - dí - a, que no po - dí - a na - ve - gar.

CD 6-6
El tilingo lingo...........Folk Song from Mexico

CD 6-7
La bamba...........Folk Song from Mexico

It sat for one, two, three, four, five, six, sev-en weeks there in the har-bor.
Pa-sa-ron u - na, dos, tres, cua-tro, cin - co, seis, sie - te se-ma-nas.

It sat for one, two, three, four, five, six, sev-en weeks there in the har-bor.
Pa-sa-ron u - na, dos, tres, cua-tro, cin co, seis, sie te se-ma-nas.

It sat for one, two, three, four, five, six, sev-en weeks there in the har-bor.
Pa-sa-ron u - na, dos, tres, cua-tro, cin - co, seis, sie - te se-ma-nas.

It was so ti-ny, so ve-ry ti-ny, it could not e-ven sail a-way.
Y el bar-qui-to, que no po-dí - a, que no po-dí - a na-ve-gar.

Cinco de Mayo

Cinco de Mayo (fifth of May) is a holiday which marks the anniversary of a famous battle in Mexico. This song about the beauty of Mexico is one that might be sung at a Cinco de Mayo celebration.

Así es mi tierra
CD 6-8, 9

Words and Music by Ignacío Fernández Esperón

A - sí es mi tie - rra, mo - re - ni - ta y lu - mi - no - sa;

a - sí es mi tie - rra, tie - ne el al - ma he - cha de a - mor.

A - sí es mi tie - rra, a - bun - dan - te y ge - ne - ro - sa;

¡Ay, tie - rra mí - a, co - mo es gra - to tu ca - lor!

© Ignacío Fernández Esperón

Sandra Longoria Glover is an educator, supervisor of music teachers, and an author for *The Music Connection*. Listen as she talks about her career in music.

Careers in Music **CD 6-10**

........Sandra Longoria Glover

Sus al-bo-ra-das tan lle-ni-tas, de a-le-grí-a.

Sus se-re-na-tas tan pro-pi-cias al a-mor.

A-sí es mi tie-rra, flor de la me-lan-co-lí-a.

¡Ay, tie-rra mí-a, co-mo es gra-to tu ca-lor! _____

A MUSICAL MARKET

Listen for the musical instruments named in this song. Then name some other instruments and make up your own verse to add on to the song.

The Market of San José (En la Pulga de San José)

English Words by Kim Williams   *Folk Song from Latin America*   **CD 6-11, 12**

In the mar - ket of San Jo - sé,
En la Pul - ga de San Jo - sé

oh, I bought a fine gui - tar,
yo com - pré u - na gui - ta - rra,

tar - a, tar - a, tar, a fine gui - tar.
ta - ra, ta - ra, ta - rra, la gui - ta - rra.

REFRAIN

Won't you go, won't you go
Va - ya u - sted, va - ya u - sted

to the mar - ket of San Jo - sé?
a la Pul - ga de San Jo - sé.

Won't you go, won't you go
Va - ya u - sted, va - ya u - sted

to the mar - ket of San Jo - sé?
a la Pul - ga de San Jo - sé.

2. In the market of San José,
   oh, I bought a clarinet,
   net-a, net-a, net, a clarinet,
   tar-a, tar-a, tar, a fine guitar. *Refrain*

3. In the market of San José,
   oh, I bought a violin,
   lin, lin, lin, a violin,
   net-a, net-a, net, a clarinet,
   tar-a, tar-a, tar, a fine guitar. *Refrain*

2. *En la Pulga de San José,*
   yo compré un clarinete,
   nete, nete, nete, el clarinete,
   tara, tara, tarra, la guitarra. Refrain

3. *En la Pulga de San José,*
   yo compré un violín,
   lin, lin, lin, el violín,
   nete, nete, nete, el clarinete,
   tara, tara, tarra, la guitarra. Refrain

Cradle Song

How would you sing a lullaby?
Would you sing it loud or soft?
Slow or fast?

Now Sleep, Little Fellow (Dormite, niñito)

CD 6-13

Folk Song from El Salvador

Now sleep, lit-tle fel - low,   Sleep safe in your cra - dle;
Dor - mi - te, ni - ñi - to,   No llo - res, chi-qui - to,

The shad-ows of ev - 'ning   Creep o - ver the gar - den,
Ven-drán an-ge - li - tos,   Las som-bras de no - che,

The rays of the moon - light,   Like fine threads of sil - ver,
Ray - i - tos de pla - ta,   Ray - i - tos de pla - ta,

Will shine on   the ba - by   A - sleep in his cra - dle.
A - lum-bran a mi   ni - ño,   Que_es-tá en la cu - na.

The morn-ing will come soon   With blue sky and sun - shine,
Ray - i - tos del sol, ___   *El cie - lo   a - zul* ___

The birds will a - wak - en   To   sing their sweet song.
De - jan de dor - mir ___   *Y em - pie - zan a vi - vir,*

So sleep, lit - tle fel - low,   While stars in   the   dark skies
Dor - mi - te, ni - ñi - to,   *Con o - jos de dia - man - tes,*

Are twink-ling a - bove you   like flow - ers of heav - en.
Es - tre - llas bri - llan - tes, *Flo - ri - do el cie - lo.*

Hawaiian Breezes

The hala is a kind of tree found in Hawaii. This song describes the hala trees swaying in the breeze. Listen for the swaying motion in the music.

Lovely Hala Trees (Nani Wale Na Hala)

CD 6-14

English Words by Alice Firgau   Folk Song from Hawaii

Love - ly are the ha - la trees, __ E - a, e - a.
Near Ha - e - na ha - las grow, __ E - a, e - a.

Sway - ing by the gen - tle seas. __ E - a, e - a.
In Na - u - e breez - es blow. __ E - a, e - a.

Nani wale na hala, Ea, ea.
O Naue ike kai, Ea, ea.
Ke oni a ela, Ea, ea.
Pili mai Haena, Ea, ea.

Try playing these percussion parts with "Lovely Hala Trees."

Sticks

Gourd rattle

What Does it Mean?

Nani wale na hala means "Lovely are the hala trees." *Naue* and *Haena* are names of places on the Hawaiian islands. *Ike kai* means "by the sea." *Ke oni a ela* means "The trees have a nice fragrance."

A KOREAN MELODY

Listen to the words of this song. What do you think the *sailboat in the sky* is?

Sailboat in the Sky CD 6-15

English Words by Aura Kontra *Song from Korea*

See the small white boat in the sky, sail-ing toward the west,
Pu reun ha nul eun-ha su ha yan jjok bae ae,

High a-bove the cin-na-mon tree where a rab-bit rests.
Gae su na mu han-na mu to kki han ma ri,

With no sails or oars it skims o'er the Mil-ky Way,
Dot dae do ah ni dal go sat dae do up si,

Float-ing a-mong the clouds as slow-ly it fades a-way.
A gi do jal do gahn da so - jjok na ra ro.

Play a Part

Try adding these accompaniment parts as you sing "Sailboat in the Sky."

Drum

Finger Cymbals

A Lovely Lady

This is a famous Arabic folk song from the Middle East. Listen for the long introduction played on a string instrument called an **oud**.

Ala Delona CD 6-16

English Words by Alice Firgau   *Arabic Folk Song*

A - la De - lo - na, A - la De - lo - na,

Fine

Through the night the des - ert __ winds are sigh - ing.

D.C. al Fine

Tell me where she's gone, My __ fair De - lo - na,
Dark and love - ly braids, My __ fair De - lo - na,

She is sweet and kind and __ brings such glad - ness.
Has she gone for - ev - er? __ Oh, what sad - ness.

In this piece, Jacques Ibert, a French composer, captures the mood of a Middle Eastern musician.

CD 6-17

Tunis-Nefta
..........Jacques Ibert

Persian Miniature   *Teheran Safaride*

Here are some parts you can add to "Ala Delona."

Drum

Tambourine

Fisherman's Song

There have been fishing villages along the rugged coast of Newfoundland for hundreds of years. Here is a song that the fishermen sing when the long day's work is done.

As you sing the song, pat your knees to the steady beat.

I'se the B'y   CD 6-18

New Words and New Music Adaptation by Oscar Brand   Folk Song from Newfoundland

1. I'se the b'y that builds the boat, I'se the b'y that sails her.

I'se the b'y that catch-es the fish And brings them home to Li - za.

REFRAIN

Swing your part - ner, Sal - ly Tib - ble, Swing your part - ner, Sal - ly Brown.

Swing your part - ner, ev - 'ry-one, All a-round the cir - cle.

2. I took Liza to the dance;
   Faith, but she could travel.
   Ev'ry step that Liza took
   Covered an acre of gravel.

3. Susan White is out of sight,
   Hiding like Jack Horner.
   Choose a lad and take him back,
   Kiss him in the corner.

Two Patterns to Play

Can you find these patterns in "I'se the B'y"? Try playing one of the patterns as the class sings the song.

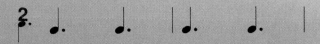

Can you accompany the song on the autoharp? Follow the chords on the music and play two strums per measure.

OUR NATIONAL

The Star-Spangled Banner

Words by Francis Scott Key   Music by John Stafford Smith

Why do we stand when our national anthem is sung or played?

Oh, __ say! can you see, by the dawn's ear - ly light,

What so proud - ly we hailed at the twi - light's last gleam - ing,

Whose broad stripes and bright stars, through the per - il - ous fight,

O'er the ram - parts we watched were so gal - lant - ly stream - ing?

ANTHEM

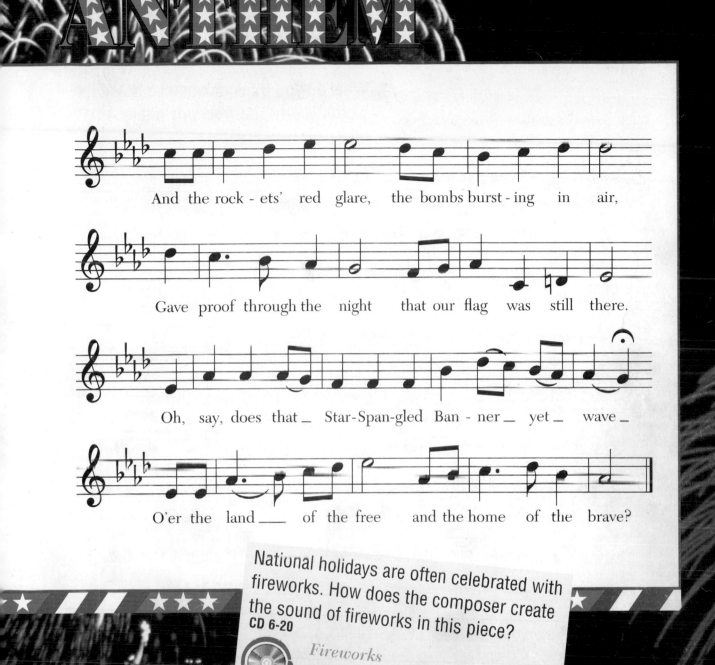

And the rock - ets' red glare, the bombs burst - ing in air,

Gave proof through the night that our flag was still there.

Oh, say, does that _ Star-Span-gled Ban - ner _ yet _ wave _

O'er the land __ of the free and the home of the brave?

National holidays are often celebrated with fireworks. How does the composer create the sound of fireworks in this piece?

CD 6-20

Fireworks

..............Igor Stravinsky

What do you think of when you read the words *liberty* and *freedom* in this song?

America

CD 6-21

Words by Samuel Francis Smith   *Traditional Melody*

1. My coun-try! 'tis of thee, Sweet land of lib-er-ty,
Of thee I sing; Land where my fa-thers died,
Land of the Pil-grims' pride, From ev-'ry moun-tain-side
Let free-dom ring!

2. Our fathers' God, to Thee, Author of liberty,
To Thee we sing; Long may our land be bright
With freedom's holy light; Protect us by Thy might,
Great God, our King!

From Sea to Shining Sea

Some of the words in this song "paint" a picture of our land. Can you paint a picture that would show America, the beautiful?

America, the Beautiful CD 6-22

Words by Katharine Lee Bates   Music by Samuel A. Ward

1. O beau-ti-ful for spa-cious skies, For am-ber waves of grain,
2. O beau-ti-ful for pa-triot dream That sees be-yond the years

For pur-ple moun-tain maj-es-ties A-bove the fruit-ed plain!
Thine al-a-bas-ter cit-ies gleam, Un-dimmed by hu-man tears!

A-mer-i-ca! A-mer-i-ca! God shed His grace on thee,

And crown thy good with broth-er-hood From sea to shin-ing sea!

Listen to "America, the Beautiful" sung in another style. How are the two performances different?

CD 6-23, 24

America, the Beautiful ....Katharine Lee Bates and Samuel A. Ward

Riding the Underground Railroad

In the days when there was slavery in the United States, there were kind people, both black and white, who formed a network to help slaves escape their terrible conditions. The hiding places they provided along the escape route became known as the Underground Railroad.

To get the freedom message to the slaves, "Peg Leg Joe" would teach them this song. The *drinkin' gourd* is the Big Dipper, which points to the North Star.

Follow the Drinkin' Gourd   CD 6-26

Song of the Underground Railroad

REFRAIN

Fol - low _____ the drink - in' gourd. ___

Fol - low _____ the drink - in' gourd. ___

For the old man is a - wait-ing for to car - ry you to free-dom

Fine

If you fol - low the drink - in' gourd.

VERSE

1. When the sun comes up and the first quail calls, _

Fol - low _____ the drink - in' gourd. _

For the old man is a - wait-ing for to car - ry you to free-dom

D.C. al Fine

If you fol - low the drink - in' gourd.

2. Now the riverbank will make a mighty good road;
Dead trees will show you the way.
And the left foot, pegfoot, travelin' on,
Just you follow the drinkin' gourd.

Music Makers:

Kim and Reggie Harris

Kim and Reggie Harris, a husband-and-wife team, make music in many places. They perform traditional songs and spirituals as well as their own compositions.

Careers in Music ....Kim and Reggie Harris

CD 7-1

Listen to Reggie Harris sing *Keep the Dream Alive.* As you listen, think about what you need to do to keep the dream alive.

Keep the Dream Alive ....Reggie Harris

CD 7-2

MARTIN LUTHER KING DAY

The civil rights movement in this country was led by Dr. Martin Luther King, Jr. Dr. King fought to secure equal rights for African American people in a nonviolent way.

"Keep Your Eyes on the Prize" is based on an old spiritual. What is the prize?

Keep Your Eyes on the Prize CD 7-3

African American Freedom Song

1. Got my hand on the free-dom plow,
2. We fought jail and ___ vio-lence too,

Won't give no-thin' for my jour-ney now.
But God's love ___ has ___ seen us through.

Keep your eyes on ___ the prize. Hold on!

...ing piece has served as a National Anthem to unite African American people.

Lift Ev'ry Voice and Sing
..........J. Rosamond Johnson and James Weldon Johnson

CD 7·4

REFRAIN

Hold   on!   Hold   on!

Keep — your — eyes   on — the prize. Hold   on!

3. Work all day and work all night,
    Tryin' to gain our civil rights.
    Keep your eyes on the prize.
    Hold on! *Refrain*

4. The only chain that a man can stand
    Is the chain of a hand in hand.
    Keep your eyes on the prize.
    Hold on! *Refrain*

Casper, the Friendly Ghost, ... a popular cartoon series in th... to the theme song from the TV s...

A Friendly Fellow

Casper, the Friendly Ghost CD 7-5, 6

Words by Mack David   Music by Jerry Livingston

Cas - per, the friend-ly ghost, The friend-li - est ghost you know,
Cas - per, the friend-ly ghost, He could-n't be bad or mean.

Though grown - ups might look at him with fright,
He'll romp and play, sing and dance all day,

1.
The chil-dren all love him so.

2.
The friend-li-est ghost you've seen.

He al - ways says "Hel - lo," And he's real - ly glad to meet cha.

Which pattern has tones that move by step? By leap?
Can you find these patterns in the song?

1.

2.

Where-ev - er he may go,   He's kind to ev - 'ry liv - ing crea-ture.

Ⓐ

Grown - ups don't un - der-stand   why chil-dren love him the most,

But kids all know that he loves them so,

Cas - per, the friend - ly ghost.

Halloween CAT

The first line of this song tells you that an old black cat hates Halloween. The last line tells you why.

My Old Black Cat Hates Halloween CD 7-7

Words and Music by Linda Williams

My old black cat hates Hal - low - een,

He shakes and quakes and cries.

He should be good on Hal - low - een,

But much to my sur - prise,

He stays in bed and hides his head,

Now, why does he do that?

"Me - ow," he says, "Me - ow," he says,

"I'm just a scare - dy cat!"

When you shuck corn, you peel off the husks—the outside covering. Long ago, people harvested corn by hand. This became a social event at which people shared stories and sang songs together. When they finished their work, they had a party.

A FALL Celebration

Shuckin' of the Corn

Folk Song from Tennessee   CD 7-8

VERSE

1. I have a ship on the o - cean, _____
2. The wind blows cold in ____ Cai - ro, _____

All lined with sil - ver and gold. _____
The sun re - fus - es to shine. _____

Be - fore I'd see my true love suf - fer,
Be - fore I'd see my true love suf - fer,

That ship should be an - chored and sold. _____
I'd work all the sum - mer time. _____

Flora L. McDowell from MEMORY MELODIES

Play a Pattern

Choose one of these patterns to play as you sing "Shuckin' of the Corn."

Sand blocks

Tambourine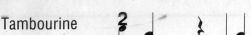

Woodblock

REFRAIN

I'm a - go - ing to the shuck - in' of the corn, _____

I'm a - go - ing to the shuck - in' of the corn, _____

A - shuck - in' of the corn and a - blow - ing of the horn,

I'm a - go - ing to the shuck - in' of the corn. _____

A Hymn for the Earth

Listen to this hymn for the earth. Can you name the instrument that accompanies the voices on the recording?

For the Beauty of the Earth
CD 7-9

Words by Folliott S. Pierpoint   Music Arranged from Conrad Kocher

1. For the __ beau - ty of the earth,

For the beau - ty of the skies,

For the __ love which from our birth

O - ver and a - round us lies,

Lord of all, to Thee we raise

This our hymn of grate - ful praise.

2. For the beauty of each hour
   Of the day and of the night,
   Hill and vale and tree and flower,
   Sun and moon and stars of light, . . .

Harvest Home

Thanksgiving began as a celebration of the end of the growing season and a successful harvest of the crops. What do you do to celebrate Thanksgiving?

Come, Ye Thankful People, Come
CD 7-10

Words by Henry Alford   Music by George J. Elvey

1. Come, ye thank-ful peo-ple, come, Raise the song of har-vest home;
2. All the bless-ings of the field, All the stores the gar-dens yield;

All is safe-ly gath-ered in, Ere the win-ter storms be-gin;
All the fruits in full sup-ply, Rip-ened 'neath the sum-mer sky;

God, our Mak-er, doth pro-vide For our wants to be sup-plied;
All that Spring with boun-teous hand Scat-ters o'er the smil-ing land;

Come to God's own tem-ple, come, Raise the song of har-vest home.
All that lib-'ral au-tumn pours From her rich o'er-flow-ing stores.

I Will Go with My Father A-Ploughing

I will go with my father a-ploughing
To the green field by the sea,
And the rooks and crows and sea-gulls
Will come flocking after me.
I will sing to the patient horses,
With the lark in the white of the air,
And my father will sing the plough-song
That blesses the cleaving share.

I will go with my father a-sowing
To the red field by the sea,
And the rooks and the gulls and the starlings
Will come flocking after me.
I will sing to the striding sowers
With the finch on the greening sloe,
And my father will sing the seed-song
That only the wise men know.

I will go with my father a-reaping
To the brown field by the sea,
And the geese and the crows and the children
Will come flocking after me.
I will sing to the tan-faced reapers,
With the wren in the heat of the sun,
And my father will sing the scythe-song
That joys for the harvest done.

—*Joseph Campbell*

SNOWTIME!

In some parts of our country, wintertime is snow time. What kinds of things do you do out of doors in wintertime?

Winter Wonderland   CD 7-11

Words by Dick Smith   Music by Felix Bernard

Sleigh-bells ring,   are you lis - t'nin'?
Gone a - way   is the blue - bird;

In the lane   snow is glis - t'nin',
Here to stay   is a new bird,

A beau - ti - ful sight, __ We're hap - py to - night, __
He's sing - ing a song __ as we go a - long, __

1.   **2.**

Walk - in' in   a win - ter won - der land!   land!

In the mead - ow we can build a snow - man,

And pre-tend that he's a cir-cus clown;

We'll have lots of fun with Mi - ster Snow - man

Un - til the oth - er kid - dies knock 'im down!

When it snows, ain't it thrill - in'?

Tho' your nose gets a chill - in',

We'll frol - ic and play _ the Es - ki - mo way, _

Walk - in' in a win - ter won - der land!

Can you name the instrument that accompanies the singers in this listening piece?

CD 7-12

"Wolcum Yole!"
from *Ceremony of Carols*
..............Benjamin Britten

SPIN the DREYDL

Some children celebrate Chanukah with games and songs. The Spin-the-Dreydl game is hundreds of years old yet is still popular today. Listen for the rules of the game in this song.

Chanukah Games
CD 7-13

Words by Rose C. Engel and Judith M. Berman   *Music by Judith M. Berman*

VERSE

1. Cha - nu - kah's the time for games. Read - y, now be - gin!
2. Round and round the drey - dl goes, See it hop and run.
3. In a cir - cle, drey - dl, turn, Turn and slow - ly sway.
4. Fun - ny lit - tle drey - dl top, How you make me laugh!
5. Whirl - ing, twirl - ing, drey - dl, go, On one foot you dance;

Spin your drey - dl, let it go, Ev - 'ry - one join in.
When at last it stops on *nun*, Priz - es? Not a one.
If you stop on *gi - mel* now, I win all— Hoo - ray!
But if now you stop on *hay*, I take on - ly half!
Shin says I must put one in And take a - noth - er chance!

Spin your drey - dl, let it go, Ev - 'ry - one join in!
When at last it stops on *nun*, Priz - es? Not a one.
If you stop on *gi - mel* now, I win all— Hoo - ray!
But if now you stop on *hay*, I take on - ly half!
Shin says I must put one in And take a - noth - er chance!

REFRAIN

Nun and *gi - mel, hay* and *shin*, Los - er, win - ner, spin and spin!

Clap this rhythm pattern.

Can you find this pattern in "Chanukah Games"?

How many times does it occur? Try playing the pattern on the tambourine as you sing the song.

Here are the Hebrew letters found on a dreydl.

nun ‏נ‎   gimel ‏ג‎   hay ‏ה‎   shin ‏שׁ‎

Listen to *Make a Little Music for Chanukah.* What can you learn about the story of Chanukah from the words of this song?

Make a Little Music for Chanukah
.................David Eddleman

CD 7-14

The Most Famous Reindeer

"Rudolph, the Red-Nosed Reindeer" was written in 1949 and has been a favorite holiday song ever since.

Pat and clap this pattern as you sing along.

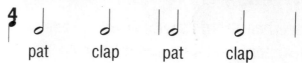

pat   clap   pat   clap

Rudolph, the Red-Nosed Reindeer

CD 7-15, 16

Words and Music by Johnny Marks

Introduction
You know Dasher and Dancer and Prancer and Vixen,
Comet and Cupid and Donner and Blitzen,
But do you recall the most famous reindeer of all?

Ru-dolph, the red-nosed rein-deer   had a ver-y shin-y   nose,

And if you ev - er saw it,   you would e - ven say it glows.

All of the oth - er rein-deer   used to laugh and call him names.

They nev - er let poor Ru - dolph   join in an - y rein-deer games.

Pattern for Four Players

You will need four players and four different percussion instruments to play this accompaniment.

Play when the picture of your instrument is shown under the note.

Feel the beat and keep the pattern going all through the song.

Then one fog - gy Christ-mas Eve, San - ta came to say,

"Ru-dolph, with your nose so bright, won't you guide my sleigh to - night?" __

Then how the rein - deer loved him as they shout-ed out with glee:

"Ru-dolph, the red-nosed rein-deer, you'll go down in his - to - ry!" ____

THE NIGHT BEFORE CHRISTMAS

Part of the excitement of Christmas is the tradition of gift-giving. Many children, wondering about their gifts, find it difficult to sleep the night before Christmas.

Sleep Well, Little Children

CD 7-17

Words by Alan Bergman   *Music by Leon Klatzkin*

1. Sleep well, lit - tle chil - dren, wher - ev - er you are;
2. Sleep well, lit - tle chil - dren, pleas-ant dreams through the night;

To - mor - row is Christ-mas be - neath __ ev - 'ry star.
To - mor - row is Christ-mas all mer - ry and bright,

Soon the snow-flakes will fall and to - mor - row you'll see
Soon you'll hear the bells ring, Time for dreams to come true

Ev - 'ry wish, one and all, wait-ing un - der the tree.
As the world wakes to bring mer - ry Christ-mas to you.

Try playing this recorder part with "Sleep Well, Little Children."

A Christmas Lullaby

How do you think this song should be sung? The headline at the top of the page will give you a hint.

The Rocking Carol

CD 7-18

Christmas Carol from Mexico

A la ru - ru - ru, my ba - by dear - est,

Oh, sleep, my ba - by, oh, sleep, my fair - est. _____

The cat - tle now have ceased their gen - tle low - ing,

The si - lence of the beasts, de - vo - tion show - ing.

A la ru - ru - ru, my ba - by dear - est,

Oh, sleep, my ba - by, oh, sleep, my fair - est. _____

Listen to two versions of another Christmas lullaby. One is sung by a chorus; the other is played by brass instruments. If you know the tunc, hum along.

CD 7-19

Lully, Lullay, Thou Little Tiny Child
........Traditional Carol from England

CD 7-20

Coventry Carol
........Traditional Carol from England

CHRISTMAS IN MEXICO

One of the Christmas Eve traditions in Mexico is the breaking of the piñata. As you listen to this song, see if you can find out why children enjoy this game.

Piñata

CD 7-21

English Words by Nona K. Duffy   *Christmas Song from Mexico*

Bril-liant lan-terns are light-ed, Our friends are in - vit-ed,

In cho - rus u - nit - ed, "¡Pi - ña - ta!"

There's no need to re-mind us, With blind-folds they'll bind us,

They'll turn and they'll wind us, "¡Pi - ña - ta!"

The pi - ña - ta, the pi - ña - ta,

Holds the can - dies for neigh-bors and cous - ins;

Can you create a percussion accompaniment for "Piñata"? What instruments will you choose?

We will whack it,   we will crack it,

And the good-ies will fall down in doz-ens.

All the chil-dren will scram-ble for can-dy,

All the chil-dren will scram-ble and shout;

All the chil-dren will grab for a cook-ie

And the oth-er good things that spill out.

Can you follow the words in this add-on song?

Children, Go Where I Send Thee

CD 7-22

African American Spiritual

1. Chil-dren, go where I send thee; How shall I send thee?

I will send thee one by one. __

Well, one was the lit - tle bit - ty ba - by, __

Wrapped in swad-dling cloth - ing, __

Ly - ing in the man - ger. __

Born, born, __ oh, __ Born in Beth-le-hem. __

2. Children, go where I send thee;
   How shall I send thee?
   I will send thee two by two.
   Well, two was the Paul and Silas,
   One was the little bitty baby,
   Wrapped in swaddling clothing,
   Lying in the manger.
   Born, born, oh,
   Born in Bethlehem.

3. . . . I will send thee three by three.
   Well, three was the three men riding,
   Two was the Paul and Silas, . . .

4. . . . I will send thee four by four.
   Well, four was the four come a-knocking at the door,
   Three was the three men riding, . . .

5. . . . I will send thee five by five.
   Well, five was the Gospel preachers,
   Four was the four come a-knocking at the door, . . .

6. . . . I will send thee six by six.
   Well, six was the six that couldn't be fixed,
   Five was the Gospel preachers, . . .

7. . . . I will send thee seven by seven.
   Well, seven was the seven who went to heaven,
   Six was the six that couldn't be fixed, . . .

8. . . . I will send thee eight by eight.
   Well, eight was the eight who stood by the gate,
   Seven was the seven who went to heaven, . . .

9. . . . I will send thee nine by nine.
   Well, nine was the nine who saw the sign,
   Eight was the eight who stood by the gate, . . .

10. . . . I will send thee ten by ten.
    Well, ten was the Ten Commandments,
    Nine was the nine who saw the sign, . . .

Listen to this Christmas
spiritual and join in singing
if you can.

*Go, Tell It on the
Mountain*
. . . . African
American Spiritual

CD 7-23

CELEBRATE KWANZAA

Kwanzaa is a time when many African American children and their families celebrate their African heritage. Children often help to prepare the decorations for the seven-day holiday.

Habari Gani is a Swahili greeting that means "What's the good news?"

Habari Gani   CD 7-24, 25

Words and Music by James McBride

VERSE

1. Win - ter ___ is here, so Kwan - zaa ___ is near,
2. Peace be ___ un to you, good things come true

Cel - e - brat - ing joy and love   as a hap - py fam - i - ly.
When you spread your joy and love   in a hap - py fam - i - ly.

Join us in our greet - ing with sev - en days of hol - i - day,
Self de - ter - mi - na - tion, ___ liv - ing as a na - tion, too.

Shar - ing all our gifts and love in a hap - py gath - er - ing.
We're all one re - la - tion and ___ live in har - mo - ny.

REFRAIN

Hap-py Kwan-zaa! Hap-py Kwan-zaa! Love and peace __ from me to you.

Ha - ba - ri Ga - ni spreads the news ____

of joy to you and asks "What's new?"

2. new?" 3. new?" "What's new?" Ha - ba - ri Ga - ni!

Japanese

New Year's Day in Japan is a very special holiday. People decorate their homes with bamboo and pine and visit their relatives and neighbors to wish them a happy new year.

New Year

A New Year's Greeting CD 7-26

Words Adapted by Katherine S. Bolt   *Music by Ue Sanemichi*   *School Song from Japan*

"O - me - de - to go-zai mas," we will bow and say,

"O - me - de - to go-zai mas," Hap - py New Year's Day.

Let us place our pine branch-es here be - side the door,

And wish our friends and neigh-bors man - y new years more.

The words of this song tell you one way to make a valentine. Can you think of other ways?

It's For My Valentine

CD 7-27

Words and Music by Linda Williams

1. I think I'll start with a pa-per heart,
   leave some space for a bit of lace,
   if there's time, I'll in-vent a rhyme,

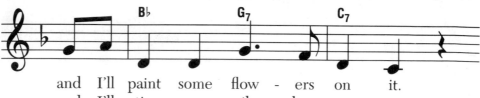

and I'll paint some flow - ers on it.
and I'll tie a rib - bon on it.
may - be e - ven write a son - net,

I'll make it all in my own de - sign,
And when it's done, it'll __ look so fine!
Or some-thing sim-ple like "Please be mine."

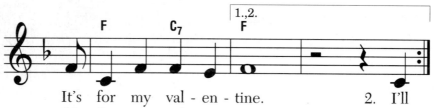

It's for my val - en - tine.   2. I'll
It's for my val - en - tine.   3. And
It's for my val - en -

tine.   Won't you be my val - en - tine?

Use this bell part to introduce the singing.

My Father's Valentine

I'm working on a valentine,
my very special own design,
a heart to give my dad tonight
(it's quite a chore to get it right).

The first time that I cut it out,
one side was thin, the other stout,
and so I tried to fix it, but
I made an error when I cut.

I wasn't careful (though I tried),
and overcut the other side,
but one more snip should do it, then
whoops! I cut too much again.

A snip off here, a snip off there,
and maybe just another hair,
it's finally done, but understand
it's somewhat smaller than I'd planned.

It's not much bigger than a bean,
the tiniest heart I've ever seen,
I guess I'll give it to him now . . .
I bet he likes it anyhow.

—*Jack Prelutsky*

A 'MUSICAL'

Never Gonna Be Your Valentine

CD 7-28

Words and Music by Linda Williams

1. I don't wan-na be your val-en-tine,
2. I'm not gon-na be your val-en-tine,
3. I might wan-na be your val-en-tine,

I don't wan-na be your val-en-tine,
I'm not gon-na be your val-en-tine,
I might wan-na be your val-en-tine,

Don't wan-na be your val-en-tine to-day!
You're not the kind of val-en-tine I like!
Don't tell a soul, 'cause you know ve-ry well,

Oh, no, I don't wan-na be your val-en-tine,
Oh, no, I'm not gon-na be your val-en-tine,
If all my friends knew I was your val-en-tine,

I don't wan-na be your val-en-tine,
I'm not gon-na be your val-en-tine,
They'd tease me and call me "Val-en-tine,"

VALENTINE

Pack up your val - en - tine and go a - way!
Pack up your val - en - tine and take a hike!
That's why you have to prom - ise not to tell!

You nev - er let me win at games,
You won't share this, you won't lend that.
But you're so mean, you won't keep still!

You laugh at me and call me names,
Won't e - ven let me pet your cat!
You'll tell them all, I know you will!

So e - ven if you beg and plead and whine,____
And yet you bor - row ev - 'ry - thing that's mine!
So e - ven though I think you're real - ly fine,

I'm nev - er gon - na be your val - en - tine!____

How many times do you find
this pattern in the song?

♩ ♩ ♫ ♩ ♩ ♪♪ ♩ ♩ ♩

THIS BEAUTIFUL

A Theme Musical by Carmino Ravosa

Social Studies   CD 8-1, 9

Words and Music by Carmino Ravosa

Ⓐ Chorus

So - cial stud - ies, so - cial stud - ies,

more than learn - ing dates and pla - ces,

So - cial stud - ies, so - cial stud - ies,

more than learn - ing names and fa - ces,

Last time to Coda

So - cial stud - ies, so - cial stud - ies.

Land We Share

B

1. Get your pen - cil or a pen,
2. It's a - bout peo - ple diff'rent as can be,

It's time for his - t'ry once a - gain.
But still the same as you and me.

Time to o - pen up your book,
It's a - bout peo - ple true and real

D.C. al Coda

Go back in time and take a look.
Who laugh and love and hurt and feel.

Coda

So - cial stud - ies, so - cial stud ies. So - cial stud - ies!

Maps and Globes

CD 8-2, 11

Words and Music by Carmino Ravosa

REFRAIN *Group 1* ... *Group 2*

There are maps and globes (maps and globes),

Group 1 ... *Group 2*

There are maps and globes (maps and globes)

All ... *(Last time)* ... Fine

That can take you an-y-where you want to go. (To go!)

VERSE *Solos*

1. You can go from the top of a moun-tain
2. You can walk from ___ Rome to ___ Chi-na,
3. You can tour the ___ whole world ___ o-ver,

From California State Map © 1993
by Rand McNally # R.L. 93-S-277

To an o - cean way on down.
See A - las - ka on a sled.
And it won't take an - y time.

From a jun - gle to a des - ert
You can tour the Ri - vi - er - a
And _____ you can trav - el first class

ritard   *D.C. al Fine*

or a - round your own home town.
and be home in time for bed.
and it won't cost you a dime.

America's Leading Import CD 8-3, 13

Words and Music by Carmino Ravosa

A - mer-i-ca's lead-ing im-port _ is peo-ple _

From a - cross the bor - ders of the sea.

A - mer-i-ca's lead-ing im - port _ is peo - ple. _

Peo - ple just like you and just like me.

They came for man - y rea - sons. _ They came from ev - 'ry-where.

They came to seek a bet - ter life, to hope and dream and dare.

They came for op - por - tu - ni - ty. They came here to be free.

They came to think and work and choose to be what they could be.

It's a Beautiful Land We Share

Words and Music by Carmino Ravosa **CD 8-4, 14**

It's a beau-ti-ful land we share.

A beau-ti-ful land out there.

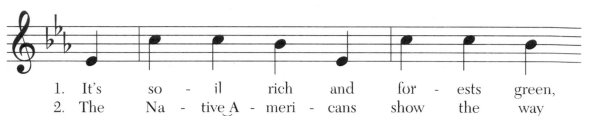

1. It's   so - il   rich   and   for - ests   green,
2. The   Na - tive A - meri - cans   show   the   way
3. It's   lakes   and   streams   and   hopes   and   dreams.

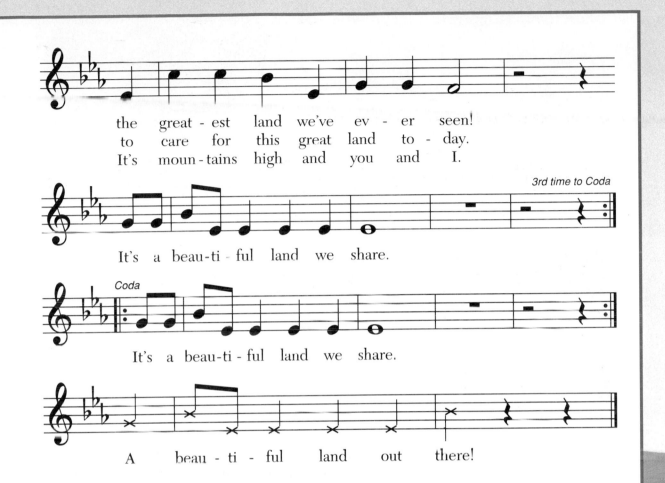

the great - est land we've ev - er seen!
to care for this great land to - day.
It's moun - tains high and you and I.

It's a beau - ti - ful land we share.

Coda

It's a beau - ti - ful land we share.

A beau - ti - ful land out there!

American Know-How

CD 8-5, 16

Words and Music by Carmino Ravosa

Thomas Edison

Came America

CD 8-6, 18

Words and Music by Carmino Ravosa

Solo first time; Chorus second time

Came A - mer-i - ca.　　　　Came A-mer-i - ca.

Peo-ple had　to get　a - long,　found to - geth - er　they were strong.
Peo-ple cleared and built this land　with their sweat and with their hands.

1.　　　　　　　　2.

Came A - mer - i - ca.　　　　Came A-
Came A - mer - i - ca.

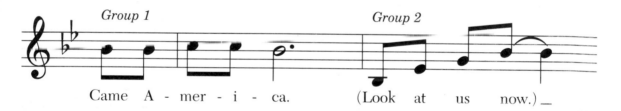

Group 1　　　　*Group 2*

Came　A - mer - i - ca.　　(Look　at　us　now.) —

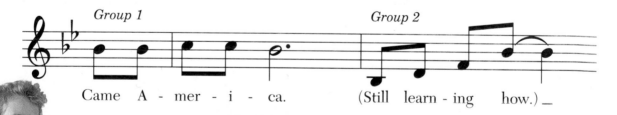

Group 1　　　　*Group 2*

Came　A - mer - i - ca.　　(Still　learn - ing　how.) —

It's in Your Hands CD 8-7, 19

Words and Music by Carmino Ravosa

Chorus

It's in your hands, the fu-ture of A-mer-i-ca,

It's in your hands, the fu-ture of this land.

It's in your hands, The fu-ture of A-mer-i-ca is in your hands.

1. Don't wait for oth-ers to think and do.
2. You've got to help and you've got to care.

Don't wait for oth-ers, it's up to you.
You've got to tell the world you are there.

READING

Many people look at a piece of music and
wonder what the notes mean. Often they wish
they could read the notes–sing them at sight
and hear how the music sounds.

This section connects you with the skill
of reading music notation.

You will learn to recognize new
rhythm patterns and solfa syllables.
You will learn how to play some notes and
songs on the recorder. And you will
learn the letter names
for those notes.

Learning to read music isn't hard to do.
And when you are able to read it, you can be
connected to music of many
times and many places.

section 3

NAME THIS TUNE

Here is the solfa notation for a song you may know.
Can you guess what it is? To find out, clap and speak the rhythm syllables.

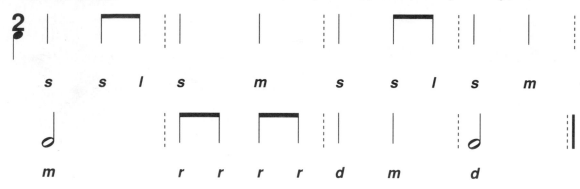

Add handsigns as you sing the solfa syllables.
Is the song written in phrases or motives?

Singing With Solfa Syllables

Practice singing these pitches and then sing the song.

d   r   m   s   l

Knock the Cymbals   CD 8-24

Play-Party Game from Texas

Knock the cym - bals, do, oh, do,

Knock the cym - bals, do, oh, do,

Knock the cym - bals, do, oh, do,

Hel - lo, Su - san Brown - o.

FROM SWING AND TURN: TEXAS PLAY-PARTY GAMES by William A. Owens. Copyright 1936 by Tardy Publishing Company. Reprinted by permission of McIntosh and Otis, Inc.

A Five-Note Scale

How many pitches are used in this scale?
Sing it with solfa syllables and show handsigns.

d r m s l

Another name for this five-note scale is **pentatonic**.

This diagram shows a pentatonic scale.

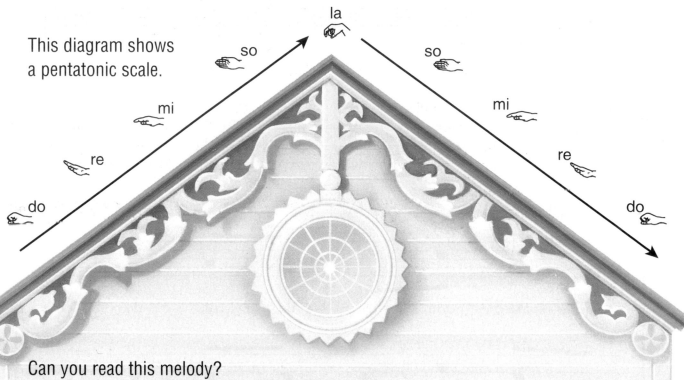

la

so   so

mi   mi

re   re

do   do

Can you read this melody?

WHERE is DO?

Great Big House

Play-Party Song from Louisiana   CD 8-25

Can you find the position of *do* on the staff?
Try singing this tune with solfa syllables.

1. Great big house in New Or-leans, For-ty sto-ries high; ___

Ev-'ry room that I been in, Filled with pump-kin pie.

2. Went down to the old millstream
   To fetch a pail of water,
   Put one arm around my wife,
   The other 'round my daughter.

3. Fare-thee-well, my darling girl,
   Fare-thee-well, my daughter,
   Fare-thee-well, my darling girl,
   With the golden slippers on her.

Two-Part Rhythm Piece

Here is a rhythm piece in two parts. Pat the beat
as you think the rhythm of the bottom part.

Pentatonic Peas?

Name the syllables used in this song. Do they form a pentatonic scale?

Old Aunt Dinah CD 8-26

Folk Song from North Carolina   *Adapted by Jill Trinka*

1. Old Aunt Di - nah hoe peas, hoe peas,

Old Aunt Di - nah hoe peas, hoe.

2. Summer's getting hotter, hoe peas, hoe peas,
   Summer's getting hotter, hoe peas, hoe.

3. Winter's getting colder, hoe peas, hoe peas,
   Winter's getting colder, hoe peas, hoe.

4. So I'm gonna leave you, hoe peas, hoe peas,
   So I'm gonna leave you, hoe peas, hoe.

From COLLECTION OF NORTH CAROLINA FOLKLORE by Frank C. Brown. Used by permission of Duke University Press.

Verse and Refrain

Here is a song for two groups of singers. One group can sing the refrain, and the other can sing the verses.

Hill an' Gully
CD 8-27

English Words by Margaret Marks *Calypso from Jamaica*

Refrain:

Hill an' gully rider,
Hill an' gully.
Hill an' gully rider,
Hill an' gully.

1. Took my horse an' come down,
Hill an' gully.
But my horse done stumble down,
Hill an' gully.
An' the nighttime come an' tumble down,
Hill an' gully. *Refrain*

2. Oh, the moon shine bright down,
Hill an' gully.
Ain't no place to hide in down,
Hill an' gully.
An' a zombie come a-ridin' down,
Hill an' gully. *Refrain*

3. Oh, my knees they shake down,
Hill an' gully.
An' my heart starts quakin' down,
Hill an' gully.
Ain't nobody goin' to get me down,
Hill an' gully. *Refrain*

4. That's the last I set down,
Hill an' gully,
Pray the Lord don' let me down,
Hill an' gully.
An' I run till daylight breakin' down,
Hill an' gully. *Refrain*

FOUR-PART CANON

Can you find the numbers that tell where each part starts to sing in this four-part canon?

Morning Bells   CD 8-28

Traditional Round

I ... II

Morn - ing   bells   I   love   to   hear,

III ... IV

Ring - ing   mer - ri - ly,   loud   and   clear.

Keep the Beat

Feel the steady beat as you clap the rhythm of this song.

Tideo CD 8-29

Play-Party Song from Texas

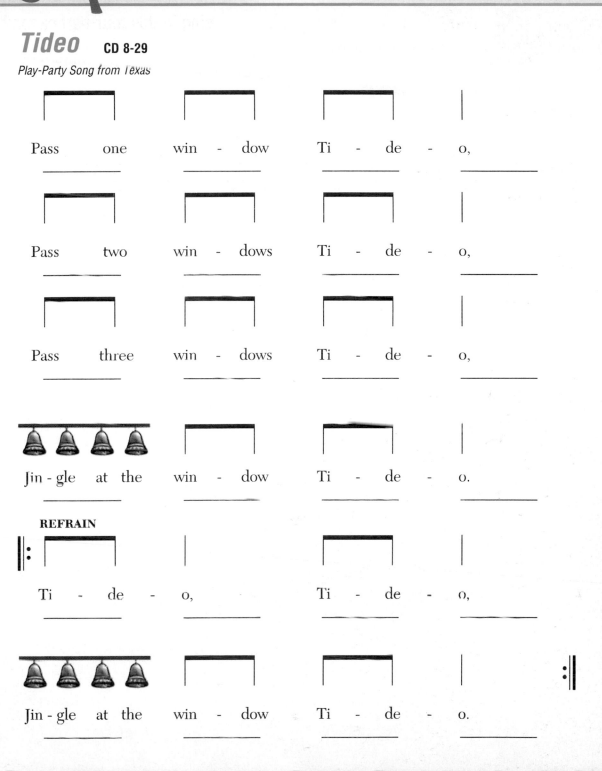

Pass one win - dow Ti - de - o,

Pass two win - dows Ti - de - o,

Pass three win - dows Ti - de - o,

Jin - gle at the win - dow Ti - de - o.

REFRAIN

Ti - de - o, Ti - de - o,

Jin - gle at the win - dow Ti - de - o.

HEADING WEST

This famous mountain pass was the main road used by pioneer settlers heading west.

Can you find the Cumberland Gap on a map?

Cumberland Gap CD 8-30

Play-Party Song from Kentucky   *Collected and Adapted by Jill Trinka*

1. Lay down, boys, take a little nap,
   Lay down, boys, take a little nap,
   Lay down, boys, take a little nap,
   Forty-one miles to Cumberland Gap.

   Refrain:
   Cumberland Gap, Cumberland Gap,
   Ooo, Hoo, Way low down in Cumberland Gap.

2. Cumberland Gap is a mighty fine place, *(3 times)*
   Three kinds of water to wash your face. *Refrain*

3. Cumberland Gap with its cliffs and rocks, *(3 times)*
   Home of the panther, bear, and fox. *Refrain*

4. Me and my wife and my wife's grandpap, *(3 times)*
   We raise Cain at Cumberland Gap. *Refrain*

A New Rhythm

Paw Paw Patch
CD 8-31

Singing Game from Kentucky

Clap the rhythm of "Paw Paw Patch" as you sing.

1. Where, oh where, is pret - ty lit - tle Mar - y,

Where, oh where, is pret - ty lit - tle Mar - y,

Where, oh where, is pret - ty lit - tle Mar - y?

Way down yon - der in the paw paw patch.

2. Come on, boys, let's go find her, *(3 times)*
   Way down yonder in the paw paw patch.

3. Pickin' up paw paws, put 'em in your pocket, *(3 times)*
   Way down yonder in the paw paw patch.

The rhythm in the color box is new.

 = 4 even sounds in one beat

Is the new rhythm in the second verse of "Paw Paw Patch"?

Conducting the Meter

Conduct meter in 2 as you sing this song.

Dinah   CD 8-32

Folk Song from the United States

No one's in the house but Di - nah, Di - nah,

No one's in the house but me, I know.

No one's in the house but Di - nah, Di - nah,

Strum - min' on the old ban - jo.

Soldier Boy

Clap this rhythm every time it appears in the song.

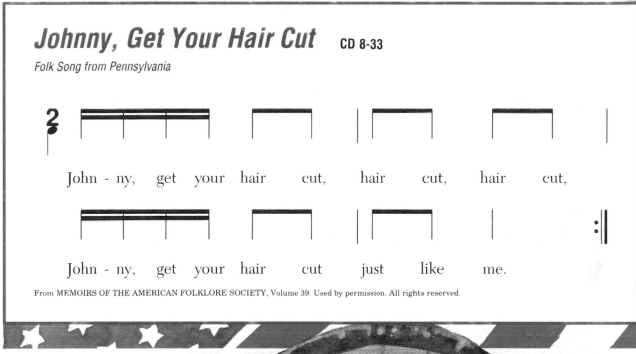

Johnny, Get Your Hair Cut   CD 8-33

Folk Song from Pennsylvania

John - ny, get your hair cut, hair cut, hair cut,

John - ny, get your hair cut just like me.

Texas Play-Party Song

"Tideo" can be performed in three different ways. Try all three.

- Sing the words.
- Sing the rhythm syllables.
- Sing the solfa syllables and show the handsigns.

Tideo CD 8-29

Play-Party Song from Texas

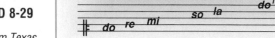

do re mi   so la   do¹

Pass one win-dow Ti - de - o, Pass two win-dows Ti - de - o,

Pass three win-dows Ti - de - o, Jin-gle at the win-dow Ti - de - o.

REFRAIN

Ti - de - o, Ti - de - o, Jin-gle at the win-dow Ti - de - o.

Just Like That

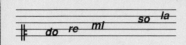

What kind of "pumpkin" face will you make at the end of this song?

Pumpkin, Pumpkin

Traditional **CD 8-34**

Pump - kin, pump - kin, round and fat,

Turn in - to a jack - o' - lan - tern just like that!

From THE SONG GARDEN by Carol Quimby Heath. Published by the Kodály Musical Training Institute. Used by permission.

Tap this ostinato as you sing.

L R L R L R

A PIECE for TWO GROUPS

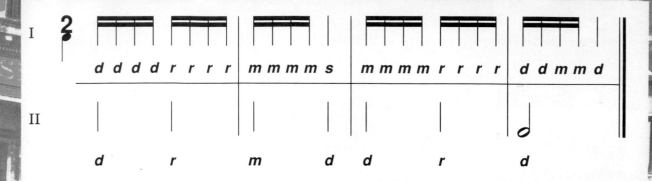

Clap the rhythm of this melody.

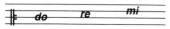

A New Sound

There is a note missing in the notation of this melody. Is the missing pitch higher or lower than *do*?

Phoebe CD 8-35

Folk Song from North Carolina

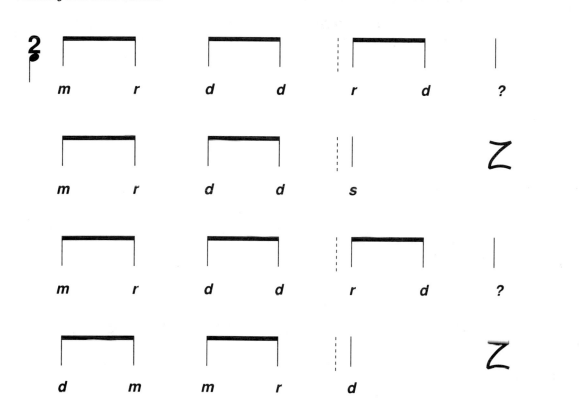

From FOLK SONGS OF THE SOUTHERN APPALACHIANS by Cecil Sharp. Used courtesy of Oxford University Press.

Trace the Shape

This song is shown in solfa notation.
Use your finger to trace the shape of the melody.
Can you show the handsign for the new sound?

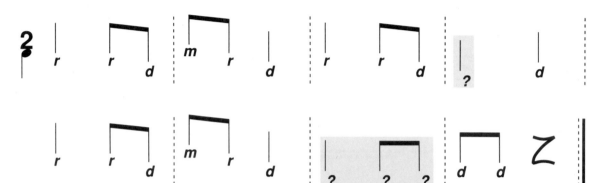

Poor Little Kitty Cat CD 8-37

Folk Song from North Carolina

r r d | m r d | r r d | ? d
r r d | m r d | ? ? ? | d d

Tune Detective

Does the new sound match any other pitch that you know?

m r | d ? d | m down | s l cap - tain
Don't let | your watch run

From SOUTH TEXAS WORK SONGS by Gates Thomas. Published by the Texas Folklore Society. All rights reserved. Used by permission.

Singing Low LA

Here is the first phrase of "Phoebe," shown with handsigns. Practice singing the phrase using handsigns and solfa syllables.

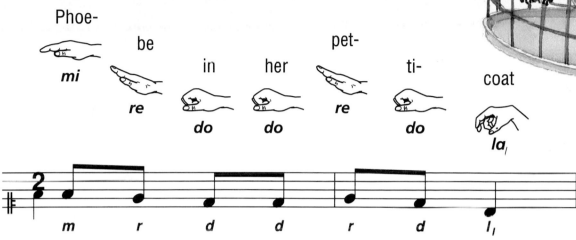

Phoe-
mi

be
re

in
do

her
do

pet-
re

ti-
do

coat
la,

m   r   d   d   r   d   l,

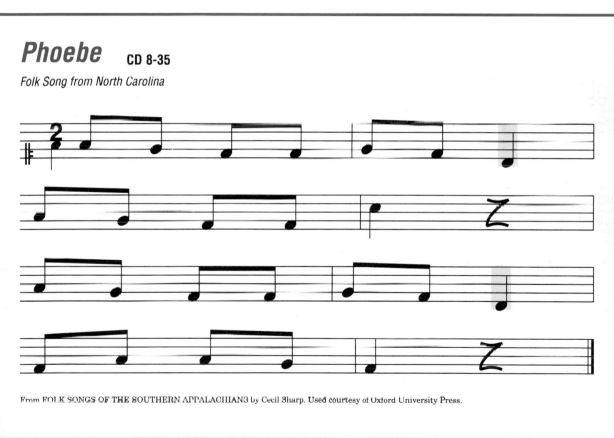

Phoebe   CD 8-35

Folk Song from North Carolina

From FOLK SONGS OF THE SOUTHERN APPALACHIANS by Cecil Sharp. Used courtesy of Oxford University Press.

Tune Detective

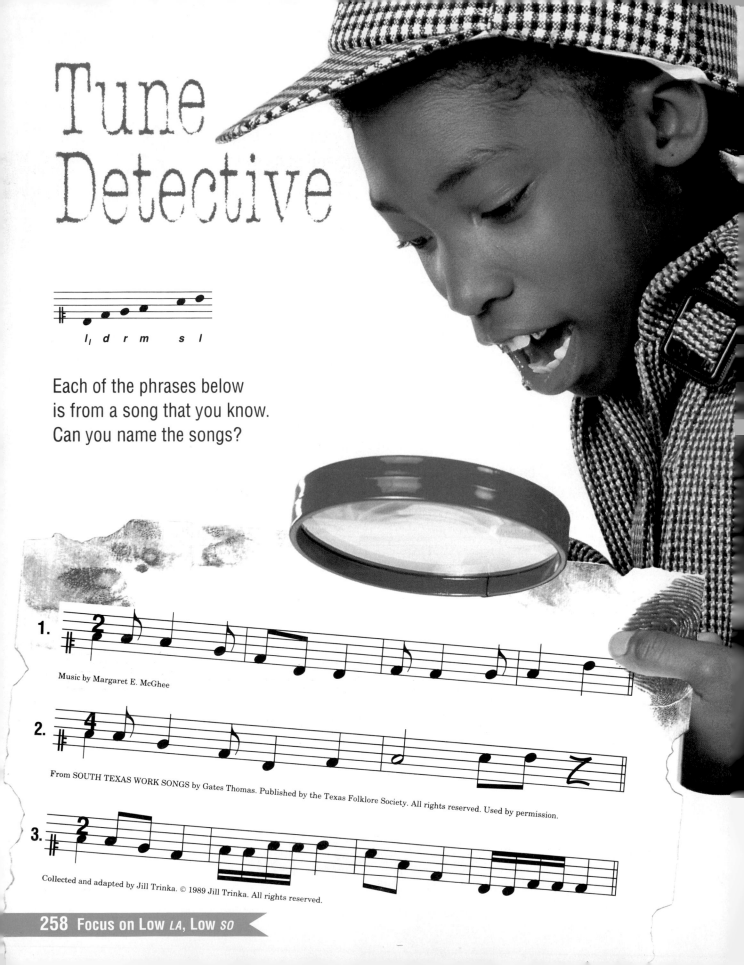

l, d r m s l

Each of the phrases below
is from a song that you know.
Can you name the songs?

1.

Music by Margaret E. McGhee

2.

From SOUTH TEXAS WORK SONGS by Gates Thomas. Published by the Texas Folklore Society. All rights reserved. Used by permission.

3.

Collected and adapted by Jill Trinka. © 1989 Jill Trinka. All rights reserved.

Tap the BEAT

Read the Rhythm

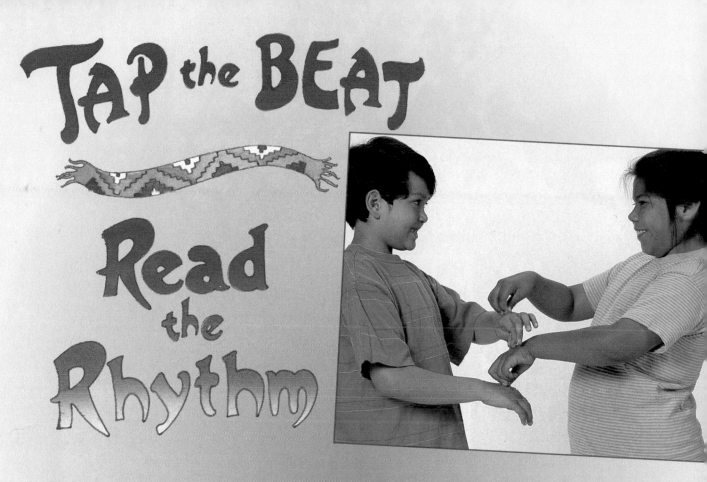

Tap a steady beat as you read the rhythm of this song. Next sing the song with the words. Now sing with solfa syllables.

Hosisipa   CD 8-38

Sioux Gamo Song

Ho - si - si - pa,   ho - si - si - pa,   ho - si - si - pa,   ho - si.

From SING IT YOURSELF by Louise Bradford © 1978 Alfred Publishing Company. Used by permission of the publisher.

Countermelody

Ho   si.

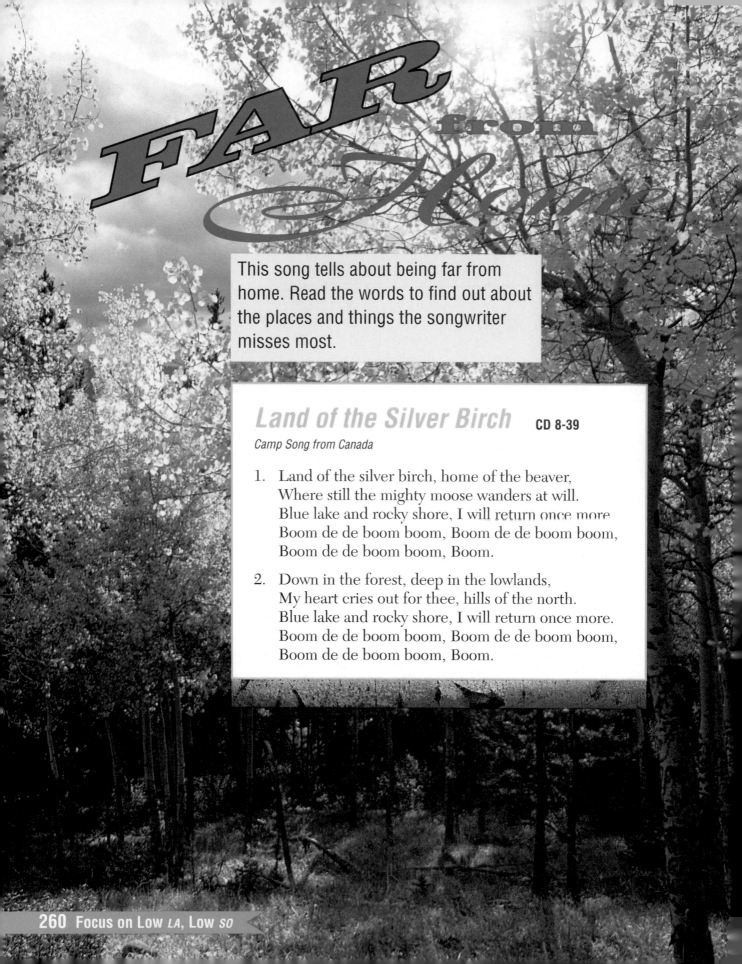

This song tells about being far from home. Read the words to find out about the places and things the songwriter misses most.

Land of the Silver Birch

CD 8-39

Camp Song from Canada

1. Land of the silver birch, home of the beaver,
   Where still the mighty moose wanders at will.
   Blue lake and rocky shore, I will return once more
   Boom de de boom boom, Boom de de boom boom,
   Boom de de boom boom, Boom.

2. Down in the forest, deep in the lowlands,
   My heart cries out for thee, hills of the north.
   Blue lake and rocky shore, I will return once more.
   Boom de de boom boom, Boom de de boom boom,
   Boom de de boom boom, Boom.

CALL and RESPONSE

Here is a song for a leader and a group of singers. Look at the notation. What can you discover about the part the group sings?

Before Dinner

Folk Song from Zaire **CD 8-40**

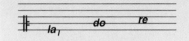

Solo   *Chorus*

First we go to hoe our gar - den, Ya, ya, ya, ya.
Next we car - ry jugs of wa - ter, Ya, ya, ya, ya.

Solo   *Chorus*

Then we pound the yel - low corn, Ya, ya, ya, ya.
Then we stir our pots of mush, Ya, ya, ya, ya.

Solo   *Chorus*

Now we eat, come ga-ther 'round the camp-fire, Ya, ya, ya, ya.

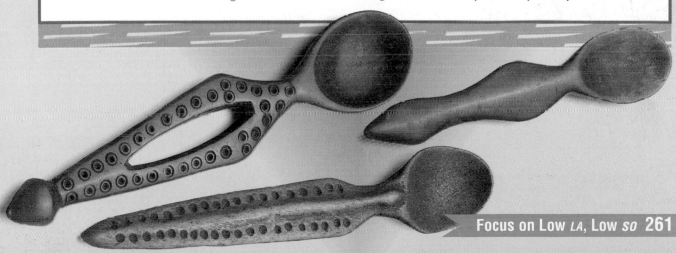

This song uses a new sound. It is lower than *la₁*. Look through the notation. Can you find the new solfa syllables?

Grinding Corn CD 8-41

Hopi Corn Song

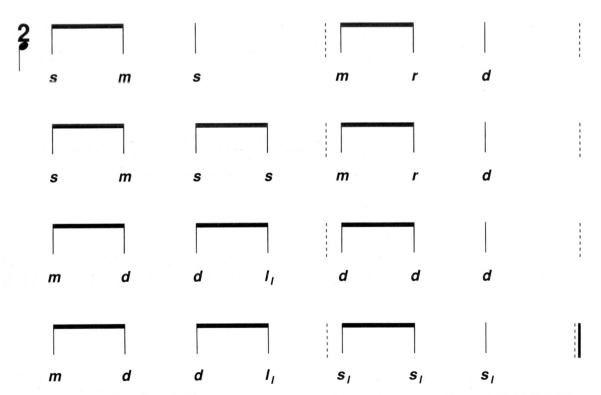

A New Note
LOW SO

Look at the color box and find the new note on the staff.

Can you find low *so* in "Alabama Gal"?

Alabama Gal   CD 8-42

Folk Song from Alabama

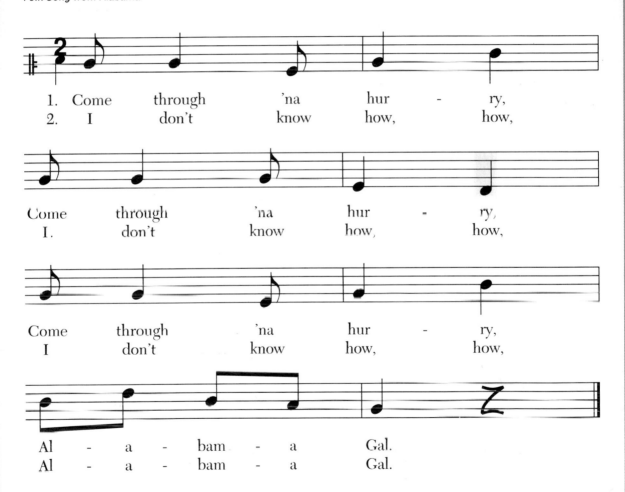

1. Come through 'na hur - ry,
2. I don't know how, how,

Come through 'na hur - ry,
I. don't know how, how,

Come through 'na hur - ry,
I don't know how, how,

Al - a - bam - a Gal.
Al - a - bam - a Gal.

3. I showed you how, how, *(3 times)*
   Alabama Gal.

4. Ain't I rock candy, *(3 times)*
   Alabama Gal?

Rhythm Detective

Tap the rhythm of the words as you sing this song.

Melchior and Balthazar CD 8-43

English Words by Emily Vidal   *Folk Song from France*

1. Melchior and Balthazar
    Went upon a journey, went upon a journey;
    Melchior and Balthazar
    Went upon a journey far with King Gaspar.

2. When they came to Bethlehem,
    They opened up the baskets, opened up the baskets;
    When they came to Bethlehem,
    They opened up the baskets they had brought with them.

3. Then they ate some cabbage soup.
    They were very hungry, oh, so very hungry;
    Then they ate some cabbage soup.
    They were just as hungry as they could be.

Which of the rhythm parts shown below matches
the rhythm of the words, part I or part II?

RING THE BELLS

Clap the rhythm of the melody
as you sing this song.

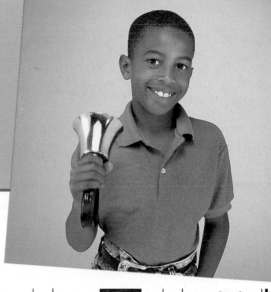

Ring, Bells   CD 8-44

Traditional Carol from Germany

I

1. Ring, bells, sing | ting-a-ling-a-ling, | Ring, Christ-mas | bells!

II

d _____ | *d* _____ | *s₁* _____ | *d* ____
Ring, | Ring, | Ring, | Ring.

I

Christ-mas bells are | ring - ing, | All the world is | sing - ing.

II

s₁ _____ | *s₁* _____ | *s₁* _____ | *s₁* ____ | *d* ____
Ring, | Ring, | Ring, | Ring, | Ring.

I

Ring, bells, sing | ting-a-ling-a-ling, | Ring, Christ-mas | bells!

II

d _____ | *d* _____ | *s₁* _____ | *d* ____
Ring, | Ring, | Ring, | Ring.

2.   Ring, bells, sing ting-a-ling-a-ling, Ring, Christmas bells! *(2 times)*
     May our hearts be merry, Joyful tidings carry.
     Ring, bells, sing ting-a-ling-a-ling, Ring, Christmas bells!

Party in the Barn

Clap and sing the rhythm syllables of verse 1.
When you sing verse 1 again, clap the rhythm
and sing inside.

Goin' to the Party   CD 8-45

Play-Party Song from Illinois

1. Goin' to the party in the old farm wagon,
   Goin' to the party in the old farm wagon,
   Goin' to the party in the old farm wagon,
   Get up, dapple grey.

2. One spring's broke and the other one's saggin', . . .
   Get up, dapple grey.

3. One wheel's off, and another one's saggin', . . .
   Get up, dapple grey.

4. Fill up the bed with straw at the bottom, . . .
   Get up, dapple grey.

5. Come on, my beauties, let's go trottin', . . .
   Get up, dapple grey.

6. All the way home without upsettin', . . .
   Get up, dapple grey.

7. Good-bye, girls, I'm glad I met you, . . .
   Get up, dapple grey.

In this song, *do* is in the first space.
Can you find low *la* and low *so*?

Chicken on the Fence Post

Play-Party Song   **CD 8-46**

s₁ l₁ d r m s l

1. Chick - en on the fence post, can't dance Jo - sey,

Chick - en on the fence post, can't dance Jo - sey,

Chick - en on the fence post, can't dance Jo - sey,

Hel - lo, Su - san Brown - y - o.

2. Choose my partner and come dance Josey, . . .

3. Chew my gum while I dance Josey, . . .

4. Shoestring's broke and I can't dance Josey, . . .

5. Hold my mule while I dance Josey, . . .

6. Hair in the butter, can't dance Josey, . . .

7. Briar in my heels, can't dance Josey, . . .

8. Stumped my toe, can't dance Josey, . . .

From A BOOK OF NONSENSE SONGS by Norman Cazdon. Published by Abelard-Schuman, 1958.

Sing the melody of "Hold My Mule" using solfa syllables. Then clap the rhythm as you sing all three verses using the words.

Hold My Mule   CD 8-47

African American Folk Song

1. Hold my mule while I dance Jo - sey,

Hold my mule while I dance Jo - sey,

Hold my mule while I dance Jo - sey,

Oh, Miss Su - san Brown.

2. Wouldn't give a nickel if I
   couldn't dance Josey, *(3 times)*
   Oh, Miss Susan Brown.

3. Had a glass of buttermilk and
   I danced Josey, *(3 times)*
   Oh, Miss Susan Brown.

Reprinted by permission of the publishers from ON THE TRAIL OF NEGRO FOLK-SONGS by Dorothy Scarborough, Cambridge, Mass.: Harvard University Press, Copyright © 1925 by Harvard University Press, © renewed 1953 by Mary McDaniel Parker.

TAPPING RHYTHMS

Tap this rhythm with your left hand.

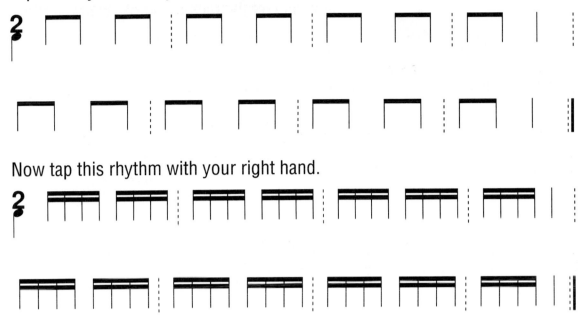

Now tap this rhythm with your right hand.

Combining Rhythms

Listen to how Russian composer Dmitri Kabalevsky used these two rhythms in a piece for the piano. Conduct meter in 2 as you listen.

CD 8-48

"Variation 5" from *Merry Dance Variations,*
Op. 51, No. 2..............Dmitri Kabalevsky

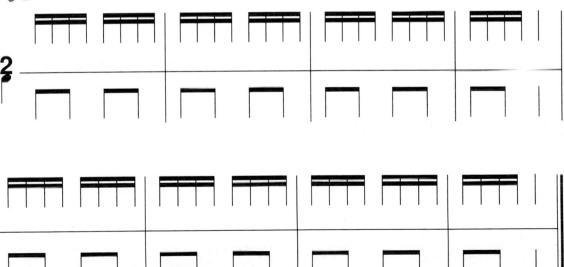

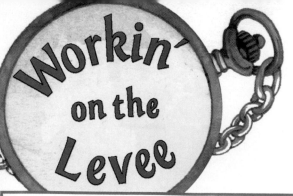

To keep a river from overflowing, workers built levees to hold back the water. The workers depended on their boss (captain) to watch carefully so they didn't work overtime.

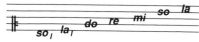

Don't Let Your Watch Run Down   CD 8-49

Work Song from South Texas

REFRAIN

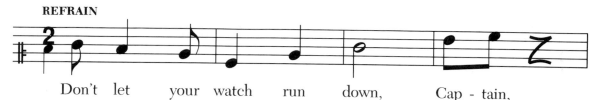

Don't let your watch run down, Cap - tain,

Fine

Don't let your watch run down. _____

VERSE

1. Wor - kin' on the lev - ee, dol - lar and a half a day,

D.C. al Fine

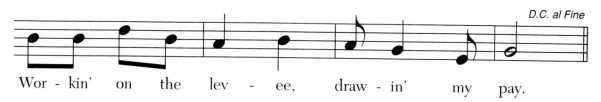

Wor - kin' on the lev - ee, draw - in' my pay.

2. Workin' on the railroad, mud up to my knees,
   Workin' on the railroad, tryin' to please. *Refrain*

3. When you see me comin', hoist your window high,
   When you see me leavin', bow down and cry. *Refrain*

LET'S PLAY THE RECORDER

Use the fingering chart below and practice playing *mi*, *re*, and *do* on your recorder.

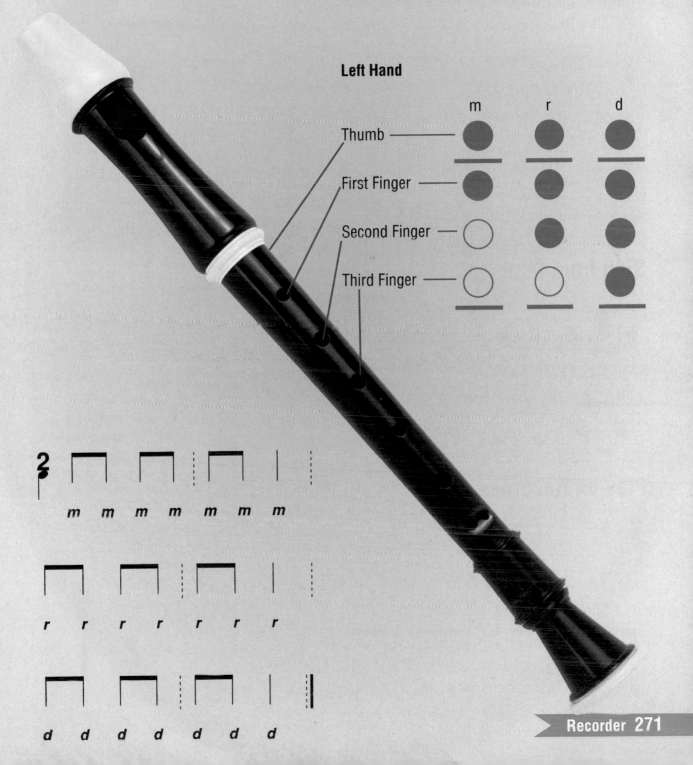

Left Hand

	m	r	d
Thumb	●	●	●
First Finger	●	●	●
Second Finger	○	●	●
Third Finger	○	○	●

2

m m m m m m m

r r r r r r r

d d d d d d d

Sing and Play

Sing and play these examples using solfa syllables.
Sing this two-line piece in solfa. Show handsigns.

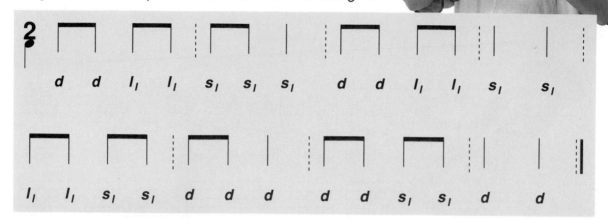

Sing from Staff Notation

Play on Recorder

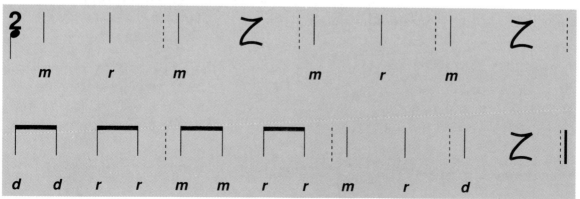

Song with Two Parts

Great Big House

CD 8-25

Play-Party Song from Louisiana

"Great Big House" is arranged for two groups of singers. Sing each part separately. Then, with your classmates, put both parts together.

1. Great big house in New Or-leans, For-ty sto-ries high; _____

1. Great, great big house, Great, great big house;
2. Old, old mill-stream, Old, old mill-stream;
3. Fare, fare-thee-well, Fare, fare-thee-well;

Ev-'ry room that I been in, Filled with pump-kin pie.

Great, great big house In New Or-leans.
Old, old mill stream, Old mill - stream.
Fare, fare - thee - well, Fare, fare - thee - well.

2. Went down to the old millstream
   To fetch a pail of water.
   Put one arm around my wife,
   The other 'round my daughter.

3. Fare-thee-well, my darling girl,
   Fare-thee-well, my daughter,
   Fare-thee-well, my darling girl
   With the golden slippers on her.

NEW NOTES FOR RECORDER

Look at the diagram below and find some new notes to play on your recorder.

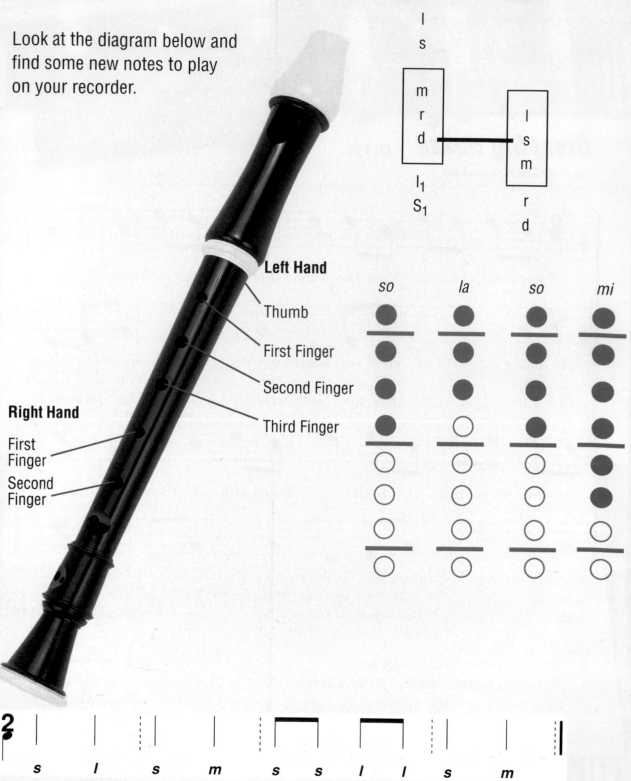

l
s

| m |
| r |
| d |

l₁
S₁

| l |
| s |
| m |
| r |
| d |

Left Hand

Thumb

First Finger

Second Finger

Third Finger

Right Hand

First Finger

Second Finger

so   *la*   *so*   *mi*

2
s   s   l   s   s   m   s   s   l   l   s   m

Read the RHYTHM ✳ Read the TUNE

Tap the beat and say the rhythm syllables. Then sing the tune in your head and show the handsigns. Sing the last note aloud.

Never Sleep Late Any More   CD 8-50

Folk Song from the United States

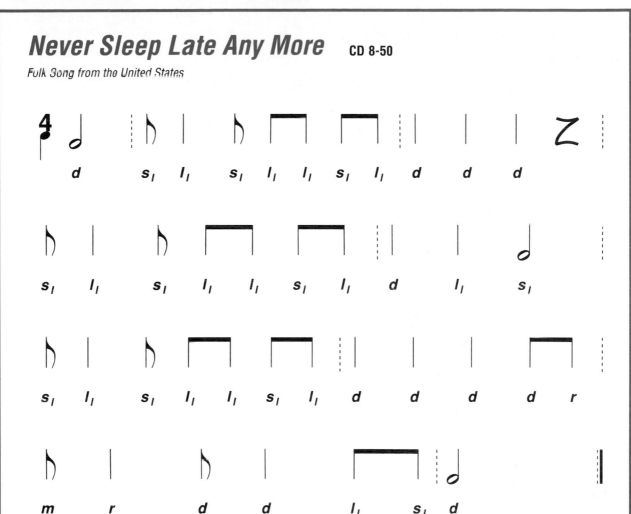

From MUSIC FOR YOUNG AMERICANS I. Used courtesy of D.C. Heath and Co.

Phrase Detective

Look at the staff below. It shows the notation for one of the phrases you just sang. Can you tell which phrase it is?

LOOK OUT!

Find a partner and try singing "Scotland's Burning" as a two-part round.

Scotland's Burning

Traditional Round   **CD 8-51**

I

Scot - land's burn - ing, Scot - land's burn - ing,

II

Look out! Look out!

III

Fire! Fire! Fire! Fire!

IV

Pour on wa - ter, Pour on wa - ter!

WHOM DO YOU LOVE?

Love Somebody

CD 9-1

Folk Song from the United States

1. Love somebody, yes, I do,
   Love somebody, yes, I do,
   Love somebody, yes, I do,
   Love somebody, but I won't tell who!

2. Twice sixteen is thirty-two, (3 times)
   Sally, won't you love me, do, girl, do!

3. Sun comes up and the moon goes down, (3 times)
   See my little girl in her evening gown.

4. Somebody come and find me gone, (3 times)
   They better leave my girl alone.

5. Love somebody, sure and true, (3 times)
   Love somebody and it may be you!

© Jean Ritchie, Gordie Music Publishing Company. Used by permission.

Tune Detective

Which example shows the melody for the phrase
Love somebody, but I won't tell who?

1.

2.

Sing and Sign

Practice singing and signing each part of the exercise below. Find a partner and sing the parts together.

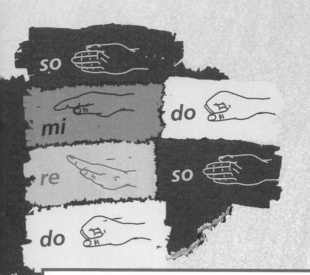

I	*d*	*m*	*s*	*m*	*d*	*m*	*r*
II	*d*____		*s₁*____		*d*____		*s₁*

I	*d*	*m*	*s*	*m*	*r*	*m*	*d*
II	*d*____		*s₁*____		*s₁*____		*d*

You can use *d* and *s₁* to make a second part for the song "Dinah."

Dinah CD 9-2

Folk Song from the United States

No one's in the house but Di-nah, Di-nah, No one's in the house but me, I know.

No one's in the house but Di-nah, Di-nah, Strum-min' on the old ban-jo.

"Silent" Singing

Sing this song "silently" by singing inside and showing handsigns. Now sing the song aloud with the words.

s₁ d r m s l

Hill an' Gully   CD 8-27

English Words by Margaret Marks   *Calypso from Jamaica*

REFRAIN

Hill an' gul - ly rid - er, Hill an' gul - ly.

Fine

Hill an' gul - ly rid - er, Hill an' gul - ly.

VERSE

Took my horse an' come down, Hill an' gul - ly.
But my horse done stumble down,

D.C. al Fine

An' the night-time come an' tum - ble down, Hill an' gul - ly.

Tune Detective

What song do you know that starts like this...

d r m d d r m d

and ends like this?

d s₁ d d s₁ d

The Music Alphabet

The music alphabet has seven letters.

A B C D E F G

Each note on the staff has its own absolute letter name. These names are determined by the G-clef on the staff.

Look at this staff and notice that the clef makes a circle around the second line. This line is called G.

If we know where the note G is located, then we can figure out the names of all the other notes on the staff.

B C D E F G A B C D E F G A

Notes going up on the staff go forward in the alphabet.

G A B C D E F G A

Notes going down on the staff go backward in the alphabet.

G F E D C B A

Play the Recorder

You can play B-A-G on the recorder. Look at the diagram below and practice the fingerings.

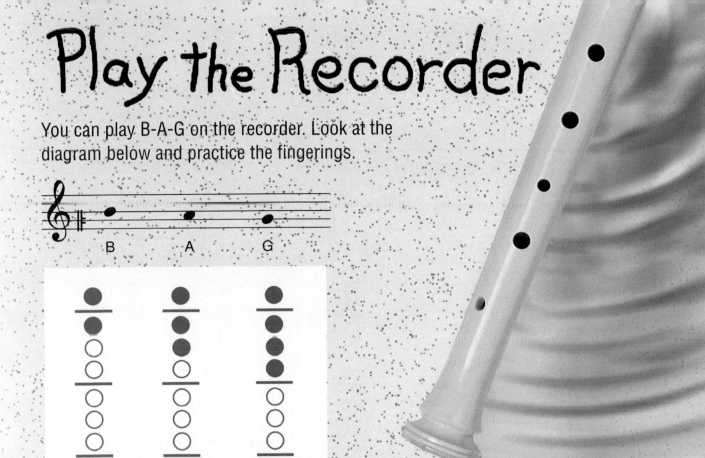

Sing the solfa syllables and then the letter names as you finger the notes on your recorder.

Sing the same melody, but use C as *do*. Sing with solfa syllables and then letter names.

DO in Three Places

Use the fingering position on your recorder to sight-read "Hosisipa." You will be reading *m, r, d,* and *l₁* in three different places on the staff. Sing the solfa syllables as you practice the fingerings.

If G = *do*, then

If C = *do*, then

If F = *do*, then

From SING IT YOURSELF by Louis Bradford © 1978 Alfred Publishing Company. Used by permission of the publisher.

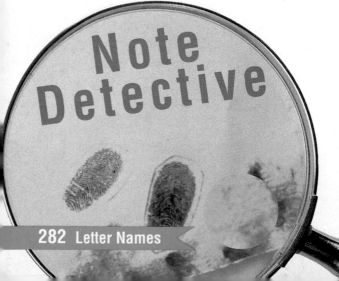

Note Detective

There is one note that is used in each of the three examples. Can you find it? What is the letter name of the note?

What solfa-syllable name does the note A have when

1. G = *do*?   **2.** C = *do*?   **3.** F = *do*?

Conduct meter in 2 and say rhythm syllables.
Sing with handsigns and solfa syllables.

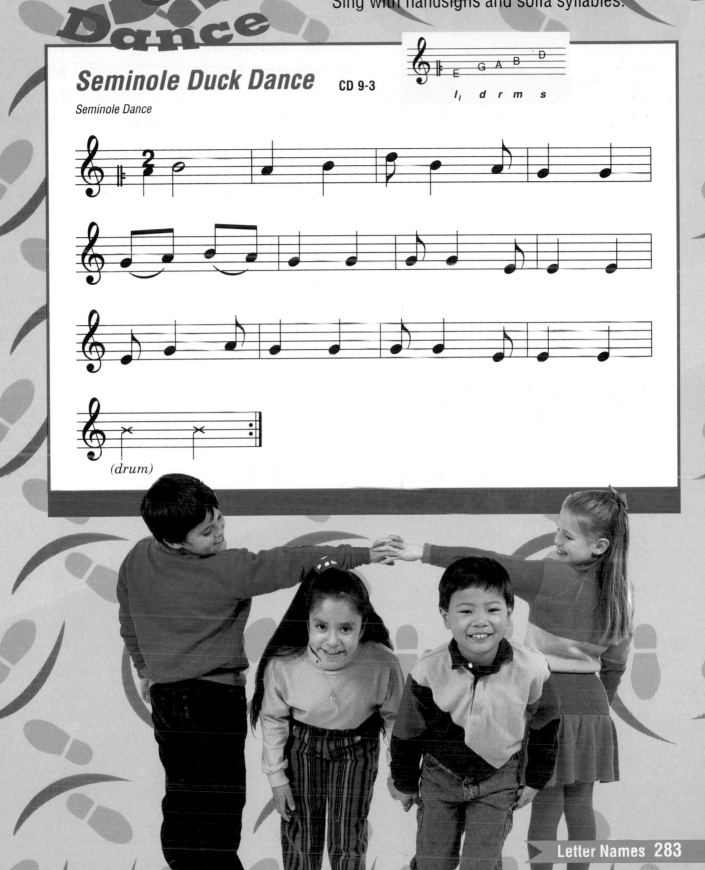

Seminole Duck Dance

CD 9-3

Seminole Dance

(drum)

Singing in Canon

Sing this song with solfa syllables.
Then find a partner and sing in canon.

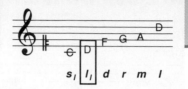

Canoe Song CD 9-4

Words and Music by Margaret E. McGhee

My pad - dle's keen and bright, Flash-ing with sil - ver.

Fol - low the wild goose flight, Dip, dip and swing.

PARTNER SONGS

Partner songs are two songs that can be sung together. "Canoe Song" and "Land of the Silver Birch" can be sung as partner songs.

Land of the Silver Birch   CD 8-39

Camp Song from Canada

Land of the sil - ver birch, home of the bea - ver,

Where still the might - y moose wan - ders at will.

Blue lake and rock - y shore, I will re - turn once more.

Boom de de boom boom, Boom de de boom boom, Boom de de boom boom,

Boom.

TALL and MIGHTY

In the Forest   CD 9-5

English Words by Jill Trinka   *Traditional Melody from Africa*

1. In the for - est dark and qui - et,

In the for - est dark and qui - et,

Here I sit in won - der,

Here I sit in peace.

2. Oh, the trees are tall and mighty,
   Oh, the trees are tall and mighty,
   Reaching up and outward,
   Reaching to the sky.

Recorder Duet

Music by Zoltán Kodály   Arranged by Jill Trinka

From 333 Elementary Exercises (#167) by Zoltán Kodály. Copyright 1941 by Zoltán Kodály. Copyright renewed. English Edition © Copyright 1963 by Boosey & Co., Ltd. Reprinted by permission of Boosey & Hawkes, Inc.

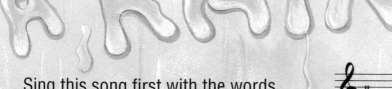

Sing this song first with the words and then with solfa syllables.

l_1 d r s l
E G A D E

Breezes Are Blowing   CD 9-6

Luiseño Rain Chant

Breez-es   are   blow - ing,   Blow-ing clouds of   wa - ter;

On   my   face,   rain - ing,   Rain - ing   from   the   o - cean;

Breez - es   are   blow - ing,   Blow-ing clouds of   wa - ter.

Clap this ostinato as you sing.
Then play it on a drum.

You have sung songs whose ending tone is *do* or *la₁*. Can you name the final pitch in "Grinding Corn"?

Grinding Corn　CD 8-41

Hopi Corn Song

Grind-ing corn, grind-ing corn, In-dian maid-ens grind-ing corn;

God of rain and sun and sky, Send the gen-tle but-ter-fly.

From SINGING WITH CHILDREN, 2nd Edition, by Robert and Vernice Nye, Neva Aubin and George Kyme. © 1970, 1962 by Wadsworth Publishing Company Inc. Used by permission of the publisher.

Sing the *so*-pentatonic scale: s_1, l_1, d, r, m, s.

s_1　l_1　d　r　m　s
D　E　G　A　B　D

Yoop Biddy　CD 9-7

Here is another melody that ends on s_1.

Plantation Song from the Southern United States

1.　2.

From SING IT YOURSELF by Louis Bradford. © 1978 Alfred Publishing Company. Used by permission of the publisher.

Create an OSTINATO

Tap a steady beat as you sing "Raccoon Dance Song." Create an ostinato for this song.

Raccoon Dance Song CD 9-8

Traditional Algonquin Song

From SING IT YOURSELF by Louis Bradford. © 1978 Alfred Publishing Company. Used by permission.

Can You Read This?

Match the solfa motives below with the motives in "Raccoon Dance Song."

1. $d - m - m - r - m - r - d - l_1$

2. $l_1 - s_1 - l_1 - s_1 - l_1 - s_1 - l_1 - s_1$

3. $l_1 - l_1 - l_1 - s_1 - l_1 - s_1 \, s_1$

4. $s - s - s - m - m - m - m - d$

Greetings

How do you greet your family and friends when you arrive home from school?

Home from School CD 9-9

English Words by David Eddleman   Folk Song from China

When the ___ sun is ___ sink - ing low,

Home - ward ___ from my school I ___ go,

There where ___ I know ___ I will find

Wait - ing, ___ fa - ther and moth - er kind.

DEAR MOTHER CROW

Song of the Crow

Folk Song from China   **CD 9-10**

In this song a young crow feeds his mother, because she fed him when he was very small.

"Caw! Caw! Caw!" says the crow to me.

He loves the old ones I can see.

Birds grow ___ old so they can't fly;

Son flut - ters out some ___ worms to spy.

Moth - er ___ dear he feeds with care.

He nev - er minds he has no share.

My moth - er dear she once fed me.

"Caw!" says the crow up ___ in the tree.

SCALE DETECTIVE

Songs that use *do, re, mi, so,* and *la* can end on different notes. The final note tells us which pentatonic scale the song uses. Which scale does the song "Frogs" use?

Frogs   CD 9-11

English Words by Betty Warner Dietz and Thomas Choonbai Park   Folk Song from China

Each frog has a sin - gle mouth,
He has two eyes and four legs.

Pin pong, pin pong, count them ___ with me.

Dur - ing time of peace, frogs do not drink.

Wa - ter lil - ies float on the pond.

Copyright © 1964 by the John Day Co., Inc. Reprinted from FOLK SONGS OF CHINA, JAPAN, KOREA, Edited by Betty Warner Dietz and Thomas Choonbai Park. By permission of the John Day Company, Inc., Publisher.

Let's Go to the Sea   (Vamos a la mar)   CD 9-12

Folk Song from Guatemala

1. Let's go to the sea,＿ tum tum,
1. *Va - mos a la mar,＿ tum tum,*

Hook some fish and fry 'em, tum tum,
a co - mer pes - ca - do, tum tum,

Mouth as red as ru - by, tum tum,
Bo - ca co - lo - ra - da, tum tum,

Bar - be - que or fry 'em, tum tum.
Fri - ti - to y a - sa - do, tum tum.

2. Let's go to the sea, tum tum,
   Catch a fish and grill it, tum tum,
   Barbecue or fry it, tum tum,
   In a wooden skillet, tum tum.

2. *Vamos a la mar, tum tum,*
   A comer pescado, tum tum,
   Fritito y asado, tum tum,
   En sartén de palo, tum tum.

Used by permission of the Organization of American States.

An APPALACHIAN Song

Notice that "Cotton-Eye Joe" is written in F-*do*. Here are the notes used in the song.

s,	l,		d	r	m
C	D		F	G	A

Cotton-Eye Joe   CD 9-13

Folk Song from Tennessee

1. Where did you come from? Where did you go?

Where did you come from, Cot - ton - Eye — Joe?

2. I've come for to see you,
   I've come for to sing,
   I've come for to bring you
   A song and a ring.

3. When did you leave here?
   Where did you go?
   When you coming back here,
   Cotton-Eye Joe?

4. Left here last winter,
   I've wandered through the year.
   Seen people dyin',
   Seen them with their fear.

5. I've been to the cities,
   Buildings cracking down,
   Seen the people calling,
   Falling to the ground.

6. I'll come back tomorrow,
   If I can find a ride,
   Or I'll sail in the breezes,
   Blowin' on the tide.

7. Well, when you do come back here,
   Look what I have brung,
   A meadow to be run in,
   A song to be sung.

8. Where did you come from?
   Where did you go?
   Where did you come from,
   Cotton-Eye Joe?

A Two-Part Song

Enjoy singing this song in two parts with your classmates.

In the Forest

CD 9-14

English Words by Jill Trinka   *Traditional Melody from Africa*

I

1. In the for-est dark and qui-et, _____
2. Oh, the trees are tall and might-y, _____

II

1. In the for-est dark and qui-et,
2. Oh, the trees are tall and might-y,

I

Here I sit in won-der, _____
Reach-ing up and out-ward, _____

II

Here I sit in peace. ___
Reach-ing to the sky. ___

I

3. In the dis-tance birds are call - ing, _____

II

In the dis-tance birds are call - ing,

I

"Come, fly a-way with me, _____ Come, fly a-way with me." ___

II

"Fly a - way, Come, fly a-way with me." ___

Wake Up

Enjoy singing this song that contains both low *la* and low *so*.

Never Sleep Late Any More   CD 8-50

Folk Song from the United States

Oh,   just let   me get   up   in   the   ear - ly   morn,

Just   let   me get   up   in   the   ear - ly   morn,

Just   let   me get   up   in   the   ear - ly   morn,   And   I'll

nev - er   sleep   late   an - y   more.

From *Music for Young Americans I.* Used courtesy of D.C. Heath and Co.

in the Morning!

Sing this song with words, solfa syllables, and letter names. Then perform the dance that goes with the song.

Turn the Glasses Over CD 3-10

Folk Song from the United States

I've been to Haar - lem, I've been to Do - ver,

I've trav - eled this wide world all o - ver,

O - ver, o - ver, three times o - ver,

Drink what you have to drink and turn the glass - es o - ver.

Sail - ing east, sail - ing west,

Sail - ing o - ver the o - cean,

Bet - ter watch out when the boat be - gins to rock, Or you'll

lose your girl in the o - cean.

PLAY THE

Using your left hand, cover the holes shown in the first diagram.

Cover the tip of the mouthpiece with your lips. Blow gently as you whisper *dahh*. You will be playing G.

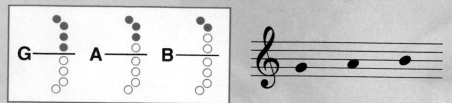

When you can play G, A, and B, you will be able to play a version of "Cotton-Eye Joe."

Practice playing two new notes—high C and high D. When you can play them, you will be ready to play a version of "Love Somebody."

RECORDER

Remember to cover the holes securely as you add new notes—C, D, E, and F.

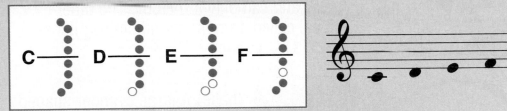

Add a countermelody to "Poor Little Kitty Cat."

Using the notes you have learned so far, you will be able to play some other songs in your book. Try one of these.

- "The Jasmine Flower," page 58

- "Scotland's Burning," page 276

- "Never Sleep Late Anymore," page 298

Read this fingering chart to discover how to play another new note—F#.

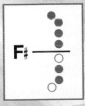

Play a countermelody on the verse of "Cumberland Gap."

SOUND BANK

BAGPIPE   A wind instrument in which one or more pipes are attached to a windbag. One or two of the pipes, called chanters, have finger holes and can play a melody. The other pipes, called drones, sound single pitches. (p. 111)   **CD 9-15**

BASS DRUM   (base) A large cylinder-shaped drum. The player can beat one or both sides with a large beater. The bass drum has a low, booming sound, which can be soft and fuzzy or loud and demanding.   (p. 106)   **CD 9-16**

BASSOON   A large tube-shaped wooden instrument with a double reed. Low notes on a bassoon can sound gruff and comical. Higher notes sound softer and sweeter.   (p. 50)   **CD 9-17**

BEAR GROWLER   A Native American instrument that consists of a heavy notched stick, a scraper, and a large drum. The player stands the heavy stick upright on the drumhead and rubs the scraper over the notched side. The vibrating drumhead makes a sound like a growling bear.   (p. 137)   **CD 9-18**

CELLO   (CHEH loh) A large wooden string instrument. The cello may be plucked with fingers or played with a bow. The cello has a rich, warm voice that can sound quite low. (p. 107)   **CD 9-19**

CLARINET   An instrument shaped like a long cylinder. It is usually made of wood and has a reed in the mouthpiece. The clarinet's low notes are soft and hollow. The highest notes are thin and piercing. (p. 108) **CD 9-20**

CONGA (KAHN gah) An Afro-Cuban drum with a long barrel-shaped body. It comes in two sizes: the small quinto and the large tumbador. The conga is struck with the fingers and the palms of the hands. (p. 261) **CD 9-21**

CYMBALS Two metal plates with hand straps. The player holds one cymbal in each hand and quickly claps them together. Cymbals make a loud, exciting metallic crash when struck together. (p. 106) **CD 9-22**

FLUTE A small metal instrument shaped like a pipe. The player holds the flute sideways and blows across an open mouthpiece. The flute's voice is clear and sweet. (p. 98) **CD 9-23**

FLUTE (wooden) An end-blown instrument made from a wooden tube. Part of the upper end of the tube is cut out to make the sound. Finger holes along the body help the player change pitches. This flute sounds very much like a recorder. (p. 136) **CD 9-24**

FRENCH HORN A medium-sized instrument made of coiled brass tubing. At one end is a large bell; at the other end is a mouthpiece. The sound of the horn is mellow and warm. (p. 98) **CD 9-25**

SOUND BANK

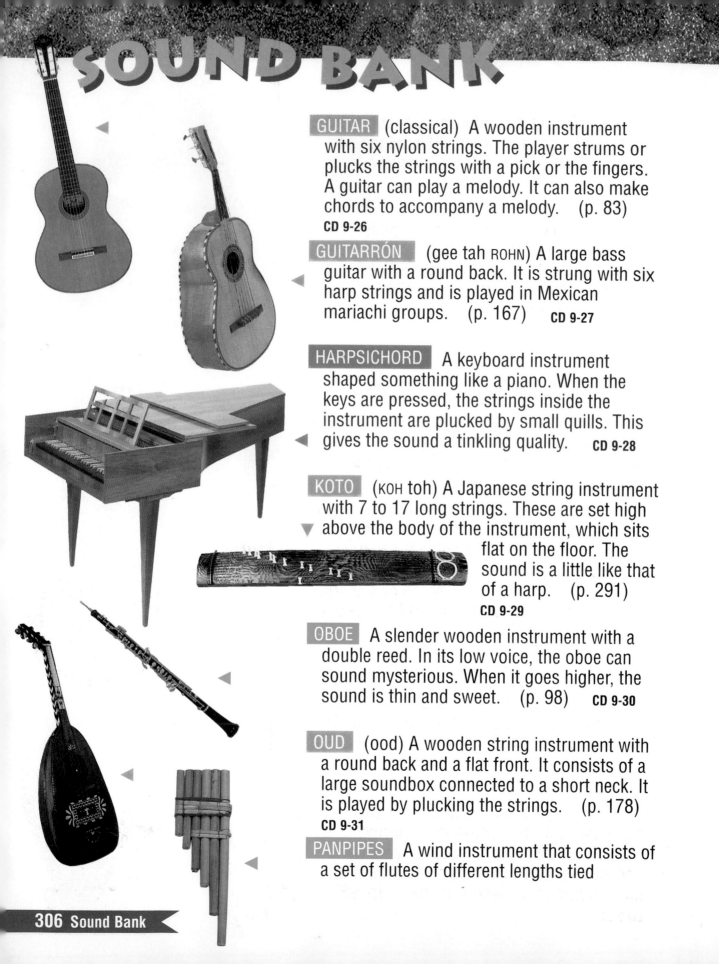

GUITAR (classical) A wooden instrument with six nylon strings. The player strums or plucks the strings with a pick or the fingers. A guitar can play a melody. It can also make chords to accompany a melody. (p. 83)
CD 9-26

GUITARRÓN (gee tah ROHN) A large bass guitar with a round back. It is strung with six harp strings and is played in Mexican mariachi groups. (p. 167) **CD 9-27**

HARPSICHORD A keyboard instrument shaped something like a piano. When the keys are pressed, the strings inside the instrument are plucked by small quills. This gives the sound a tinkling quality. **CD 9-28**

KOTO (KOH toh) A Japanese string instrument with 7 to 17 long strings. These are set high above the body of the instrument, which sits flat on the floor. The sound is a little like that of a harp. (p. 291)
CD 9-29

OBOE A slender wooden instrument with a double reed. In its low voice, the oboe can sound mysterious. When it goes higher, the sound is thin and sweet. (p. 98) **CD 9-30**

OUD (ood) A wooden string instrument with a round back and a flat front. It consists of a large soundbox connected to a short neck. It is played by plucking the strings. (p. 178)
CD 9-31

PANPIPES A wind instrument that consists of a set of flutes of different lengths tied together. Sound is produced by blowing across the open upper ends. Each flute has its own pitch. The longer the flute, the lower its pitch.   (p. 111)   **CD 9-32**

REQUINTO   (reh KEEN toh) A small guitar, similar to a ukulele. It has four strings that are plucked with a long, thin pick. The requinto often plays very fast melodies. (p. 167)   **CD 9-33**

SHAKUHACHI   (shah koo HAH chee) A Japanese wind instrument made of bamboo. The shakuhachi is played with lots of pitch bends, clicks, and flutters. It sounds like a human singing voice and can produce unusual airy sounds.   (p. 110)   **CD 9-34**

SNARE DRUM   A small cylinder-shaped drum with two heads. Snares, or strings wrapped with wire, are stretched across the bottom head to create a vibrating sound. A snare drum can make a long, raspy roll or a sharp, rhythmic beating sound.   (p. 106)   **CD 9-35**

STRING BASS   A large wooden string instrument that is either plucked or bowed. The string bass is so tall that a player must stand up or sit on a high stool to play it. The voice of the string bass is deep, dark, and sometimes rumbling.   (p. 90)   **CD 9-36**

TIMPANI   Large pot-shaped drums, also called kettledrums. Unlike most drums, timpani can be tuned to notes of the scale. The timpani's voice can be a loud boom, a quiet thump, or a distant rumble.   (p. 98)
CD 9-37

SOUND BANK

TROMBONE A fairly large brass instrument with a large bell at one end of the tubing and a long curved slide. The trombone can be loud and brilliant, but its soft voice is mellow. (p. 67) **CD 9-38**

TRUMPET A small brass instrument with a bell at one end of its coiled tubing. The trumpet's voice can be loud and bright but can also sound warm and sweet. (p. 67) **CD 9-39**

TUBA A very large brass instrument with a wide bell at one end of coiled tubing. The tuba's low notes are soft and dark-sounding. The higher ones are full and warm. (p. 109) **CD 9-40**

VIOLA (vee OH luh) A wooden string instrument that looks like a large violin. The viola is either bowed or plucked. The sound of the viola is deeper, richer, and darker than that of the violin. (p. 107) **CD 9-41**

VIOLIN A small wooden string instrument that is held under the player's chin. The violin plays sounds from low to very high. A good player can create many unusual and interesting sounds on the violin. (p. 98) **CD 9-42**

XYLOPHONE A keyboard of wooden bars played with mallets. The xylophone has a bright, brittle sound. (p. 106) **CD 9-43**

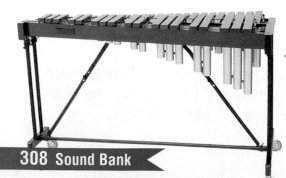

GLOSSARY

AB form (p. 62)   A musical plan that has two different parts, or sections.

ABA form (p. 80)   A musical plan that has three sections. The first and last sections are the same. The middle section is different.

accompaniment (p. 59)   Music that supports the featured performers.

ballad (p. 160)   In music, a song that tells a story.

chord (p. 40)   A group of three or more different tones played or sung at the same time.

chorus (p. 102)   A group of singers performing as a unit.

coda (p. 49)   A short section at the end of a piece of music that brings it to a close.

composer (p. 60)   A person who makes up pieces of music by putting sounds together in his or her own way.

contrast (p. 83)   Two or more things that are different. In music, slow is a contrast to fast; Section A is a contrast to Section B.

countermelody (p. 90)   A melody that is played or sung at the same time as another melody.

dynamics   The loudness and softness of sound.

form (p. 64)   The overall plan of a piece of music.

harmony (p. 40)   Two or more different tones sounding at the same time.

improvise (p. 33)   To make up music as it is being performed.

introduction (p. 135)   In a song, music that is played before the singing begins.

leap (p. 34)   A move from one tone to another that skips over the tones in between.

lullaby (p. 49)   A quiet song, often sung when rocking a child to sleep.

melody (p. 27)   A line of single tones that move upward, downward, or repeat.

melody pattern (p. 33)   An arrangement of pitches into a small grouping, usually occurring several times in a piece.

meter (p. 20)   The way the beats of music are grouped, often in sets of two or in sets of three.

mood (p. 38)   The feeling that a piece of music gives. The mood of a lullaby is quiet and gentle.

notes (p. 30)   Symbols for sound in music.

ostinato (p. 40)   A rhythm pattern or a melody pattern that repeats.

partner songs (p. 42)   Two or more different songs that can be sung at the same time to create harmony.

GLOSSARY

phrase (p. 52)   A musical "sentence." Each *phrase* expresses one thought.

refrain (p. 144)   The part of a song that repeats, using the same melody and words.

repeated tones (p. 28)   Two or more tones in a row that have the same sound.

repetition (p. 83)   Music that is the same, or almost the same, as music that was heard earlier.

rests   Symbols for silences in music.

rhythm pattern (p. 68)   A group of long and short sounds.

rondo form (p. 84)   A musical form in which a section is repeated, with contrasting sections in between (such as ABACA).

round (p. 48)   A follow-the-leader process in which all sing the same melody but start at different times.

solo (p. 102)   Music for a single singer or player, often with an instrumental accompaniment.

steady beat (p. 6)   A regular pulse.

step (p. 36)   A move from one tone to another without skipping a tone in between.

strong beat (p. 21)   The first beat in a measure.

tempo (p. 12)   The speed of the beat in music.

theme (p. 87)   An important melody that occurs several times in a piece of music.

tone color (p. 98)   The special sound that makes one instrument or voice sound different from another.

CLASSIFIED INDEX

FOLK, TRADITIONAL, AND REGIONAL

Africa. *See also* **Morocco; Zaire.**
In the Forest   286, 296
Traditional: *Lifikile Evangeli*   103

African American
All Night, All Day   82
Charles: *Ain't That Love*   103
Children, Go Where I Send Thee   214
Dett: *In the Bottoms*, "Juba Dance"   14
Do, Lord   144
Follow the Drinkin' Gourd   186
Habari Gani   216
Harris: *Keep the Dream Alive*   189
He's Got the Whole World in His Hands   142
Hold My Mule   268
Johnson and Johnson: *Lift Ev'ry Voice and Sing* (excerpt)   191
Joplin: *Maple Leaf Rag*   14
Keep Your Eyes on the Prize   190
Now Let Me Fly   78
Oh, Won't You Sit Down   102
Peace like a River   56
Traditional: *Amen*   123
Traditional: *Go Tell It on the Mountain*   215
Two Wings   34
Walk Together, Children   122

Andean
Robles: *El condor pasa* (excerpt)   111

Canada
I'se the B'y (Newfoundland)   180
Land of the Silver Birch   260, 285

Caribbean Islands
Four White Horses   28

China
Frogs   293
Home from School   291
Jasmine Flower, The   58
Song of the Crow   292

Czechoslovakia
Stodola Pumpa   12

El Salvador
Now Sleep, Little Fellow (*Dormite, niñito*)   172

England
Billy Boy   68
Traditional Carol: Coventry Carol   211
Traditional Carol: *Lully, Lullay, Thou Little Tiny Child*   211

France
Brother John   41
Melchior and Balthazar   264

Germany
Ring, Bells   265

Guatemala
Let's Go to the Sea (*Vamos a la mar*)   294

Hungary
Brahms: *Hungarian Dance No. 6*   13

Israel (Hebrew, Jewish)
Chanukah Games   204
Eddleman: *Make a Little Music for Chanukah*   205
We Come to Greet You in Peace   124

Jamaica
Hill an' Gully   245, 279

Japan
New Year's Greeting, A   219
Traditional: *Mountains Before Snow* (excerpt)   110

Korea
Sailboat in the Sky   176

Latin America
Ambos a dos   62
Market of San José, The (*En la Pulga de San José*)   170
Tiny Boat, The (*El barquito*)   166

Mexico
Así es mi tierra   168
De colores   140
Don Gato   160
First of January, The (*Uno de enero*)   66

CLASSIFIED INDEX

La raspa   84
Piñata   212
Rocking Carol, The   210
Traditional: *El tilingo lingo*   167
Traditional: *La bamba*   167

Middle East
Ala Delona   178

Morocco. *See also* Africa.
A Ram Sam Sam   88

Native American
Breezes Are Blowing (Luiseño)   288
Grinding Corn (Hopi)   262, 289
H'Atira (Pawnee)   134
Hosisipa (Sioux)   259, 282
Nakai: *Daybreak Vision*   136
Traditional: *Bear Dance Song* (Southern Ute)   137
Traditional: *Raccoon Dance Song* (Algonquin)   290
Traditional: *Seminole Duck Dance* (Seminole)   283

New Zealand
Whaka Poi   52

Norway
Oleana   156

Romania
Traditional: *Romanian Lullaby*   255

Russia
May the Sun Shine Forever   70
Traditional: *Garden of the Earth*   115

Scotland
Little Boy of the Sheep (Hebrides Islands)   64
Traditional: *Regimental March*   111

Spain
Sun and the Moon, The (*El sol y la luna*)   74

United States
Alabama Gal (Alabama)   263
Boil Them Cabbage Down   20
Bow, Belinda   43

Chicken on the Fence Post   267
Coffee Grows on White Oak Trees   24
Cotton-Eye Joe (Tennessee)   295
Cumberland Gap (Kentucky)   248
Dinah   250, 278
Don't Let Your Watch Run Down (Texas)   270
Down in the Valley (Kentucky)   55
Goin' to the Party (Illinois)   266
Great Big House (Louisiana)   243, 273
Home on the Range   146
Johnny, Get Your Hair Cut (Pennsylvania)   251
Knock the Cymbals (Texas)   241
Love Somebody   277
Lovely Hala Trees (Hawaii)   174
My Home's in Montana   148
Never Sleep Late Anymore   275, 298
Old Aunt Dinah (North Carolina)   244
Paw Paw Patch (Kentucky)   249
Phoebe (North Carolina)   255, 257
Polly Wolly Doodle   104
Poor Little Kitty Cat (North Carolina)   256
Roll on the Ground (Mississippi)   90
Sandy Land (Oklahoma)   42
Shuckin' of the Corn (Tennessee)   196
Skip to My Lou   43
Sweet Potatoes (Creole)   92
Tideo (Texas)   247, 252
Turn the Glasses Over   72, 300
Yankee Doodle   150
Yoop Biddy   289

Zaire. *See also* Africa.
Before Dinner   261

HOLIDAY, SEASONAL, SPECIAL OCCASION

December Holidays
Chanukah Games   204
Children, Go Where I Send Thee   214
Habari Gani   216
Melchior and Balthazar   264
Piñata   212
Ring, Bells   265
Rocking Carol, The   210
Rudolph, the Red-Nosed Reindeer   206
Sleep Well, Little Children   208
Winter Wonderland   202

Halloween
Casper, the Friendly Ghost   192
My Old Black Cat Hates Halloween   194
Pumpkin, Pumpkin   253

New Year's Day
New Year's Greeting, A   219

Patriotic
America   184
America, the Beautiful   185
Star-Spangled Banner, The   182
This Land Is Your Land   116
Yankee Doodle   150

Thanksgiving
Come, Ye Thankful People, Come   200
For the Beauty of the Earth   199

United Nations Day
We Come to Greet You in Peace   124

Valentine's Day
It's for My Valentine   220
Love Somebody   277
Never Gonna Be Your Valentine   222

LISTENING SELECTIONS

Anderson: *Trumpeter's Lullaby*   82

Bach: *Two-Part Invention No. 8 in F major*   7
Barry and Greenwich: *Do Wah Diddy Diddy*   9
Bates and Ward: *America, the Beautiful*   185
Bonne and Mills: *I Know an Old Woman*   153
Bozza: *Scherzo*   108
Brahms: *Hungarian Dance No. 6*   13
Britten: *Ceremony of Carols*, "Wolcum Yole!"   203

Charles: *Ain't That Love*   103
Copland: *Rodeo*, "Hoe-Down"   133
Copland: *The Red Pony*, "Circus Music"   86
Cowell: *Pulse* (excerpt)   106

Delibes: *Coppélia*, "Waltz of the Doll"   23

Dett: *In the Bottoms*, "Juba Dance"   14

Eddleman: *Make a Little Music for Chanukah*   205

Gershwin: *Preludes for Piano, No. 2* (Call Chart)   83

Harris: *Keep the Dream Alive*   189
Haydn: *Quartet in G Major,* Op. 77, No. 1, "Presto"   107

Ibert: *Tunis-Nefta*   178

Johnson and Johnson: *Lift Ev'ry Voice and Sing* (excerpt)   191
Joplin: *Maple Leaf Rag*   14
Joubert: *Rap Track 1*   11
Joubert: *Rap Track 2*   11

Kabalevsky: *Merry Dance Variations,* Op. 51, No. 2, "Variation 5"   269
Kabalevsky: *The Comedians*, "March"   76
Kabalevsky: *The Comedians*, "Galop"   76

Lapow: *Supermarket Shuffle*   10

Miller: *Big River*, "Worlds Apart"   19
Mouret: *Rondeau*   109

Nakai: *Daybreak Vision*   136

Osahanin and Ostrovsky: *Let the Sun Shine Forever*   71

Purcell: *Trumpet Tune* (Call Chart)   67
Ravel: *Mother Goose Suite*, "The Conversations of Beauty and the Beast"   96
Robles: *El condor pasa* (excerpt)   111

Schumann: *Album for the Young*, "Soldier's March"   52
Schumann: *Album for the Young*, "The Happy Farmer"   38

CLASSIFIED INDEX

Schumann: *Scenes from Childhood*, "Dreaming"   38

Shostakovich: *The Age of Gold Ballet*, "Polka"   34

Simons: *Set of Poems for Children*, "Fog"   60

Simons: *Set of Poems for Children*, "My Shadow"   60

Sterling: *Music Goes with Anything*   95

Stravinsky: *The Firebird*, "Berceuse"   50

Stravinsky: *Fireworks*   183

Susato: *Three Dances*, "Ronde" (Call Chart)   67

Tarrega: *Adelita* (Call Chart)   83

Tchaikovsky: *Nutcracker Suite*, "Arab Dance"   26

Tchaikovsky: *Nutcracker Suite*, "Dance of the Reed Flutes"   26

Tchaikovsky: *Nutcracker Suite*, "March"   21

Tickle Tune Typhoon: *East/West*   17

Traditional African: *Lifikile Evangeli*   103

Traditional African American: *Amen*   123

Traditional African American: *Go, Tell It on the Mountain*   215

Traditional Algonquin: *Raccoon Dance Song*   290

Traditional English: *Coventry Carol*   211

Traditional English: *Lully, Lullay, Thou Little Tiny Child*   211

Traditional Japanese: *Mountains Before Snow* (excerpt)   110

Traditional Mexican: *El tilingo lingo*   167

Traditional Mexican: *La bamba*   167

Traditional Romanian: *Romanian Lullaby*   255

Traditional Russian: *Garden of the Earth*   115

Traditional Scottish: *Regimental March*   111

Traditional Seminole: *Seminole Duck Dance*   283

Traditional Southern Ute: *Bear Dance Song*   137

Traditional: *America, Two Ways*   40

Traditional: *Make New Friends*   48

POEMS AND STORIES

Fog   61

How Doth the Little Crocodile   155

I Will Go with My Father A-Ploughing   201

My Father's Valentine   221

My Shadow   61

Nicely, Nicely   135

No Rain, No Rainbow   29

Peace Dove, The   125

Surprise, The (story)   32

Water-Go-Round, The   45

Weather   101

Wind, The   100

RECORDED INTERVIEWS

Careers in Music
Sandra Longoria Glover   169

Kim and Reggie Harris   189

Tickle Tune Typhoon   164

THEME MUSICAL

American Know-How   232

America's Leading Import   228

Came America   234

It's a Beautiful Land We Share   230

It's in Your Hands   236

Maps and Globes   226

Social Studies   224

SONG INDEX

A Ram Sam Sam 88 3-29
Ala Delona 178 6-16
Alabama Gal 263 8-42
All Night, All Day 82 3-21
Ambos a dos 62 2-35, 2-36
America 184 6-21
America, the Beautiful 185 6-22
American Children 130 5-6
American Know-How 232 8-5
America's Leading Import 228 8-3
Así es mi tierra 168 6-8

Before Dinner 261 8-40
Billy Boy 68 3-7
Boil Them Cabbage Down 20 1-22
Bow, Belinda 43 2-16
Breezes Are Blowing 288 9-6
Brother John 41 2-14
But the Cat Came Back 162 6-3

Came America 234 8-6
Canoe Song 284 9-4
Casper, the Friendly Ghost 192 7-5
Chanukah Games 204 7-13
Chicken on the Fence Post 267 8-46
Children, Go Where I Send Thee 214 7-22
Coffee Grows on White Oak Trees 24 1-26
Color of Music, The 98 4-4
Come, Ye Thankful People, Come 200 7-10
Cotton-Eye Joe 295 9-13
Cumberland Gap 248 8-30

De colores 140 5-13
Deep in the Heart of Texas 132 5-8
Dinah 250, 278 8-32, 9-2
Do, Lord 144 5-17
Don Gato 160 6-1, 6-2
Don't Let Your Watch Run Down 270 8-49
Down in the Valley 55 2-28

Each of Us Is a Flower 126 5-3
El sol y la luna (The Sun and the Moon) 74
  3-14

En la Pulga de San José (The Market of San José)
  170 6-12
Everything Is Beautiful 120 4-25

First of January, The (Uno de enero) 66 3-3
Follow the Drinkin' Gourd 186 6-26
For the Beauty of the Earth 199 7-9
Four White Horses 28 1-30
Frogs 293 9-11

Garden Song 118 4-24
Goin' to the Party 266 8-45
Great Big House 243, 273 8-25
Grinding Corn 262, 289 8-41

Habari Gani 216 7-24
H'Atira 134 5-10
Here Comes a Bluebird 240 8-23
He's Got the Whole World in His Hands 142 5-14
Hey, Dum Diddeley Dum 94 4-1
Hill an' Gully 245, 279 8-27
Hold My Mule 268 8-47
Home from School 291 9-9
Home on the Range 146 5-19
Hosisipa 250, 282 8-38

I Care About Being Me 6 1-3
I Know an Old Lady 152 5-23
If I Only Had a Brain 158 5-28
In the Forest 286, 296 9-5, 9-14
I'se the B'y 180 6-18
It's a Beautiful Day 36 2-8
It's a Beautiful Land We Share 230 8-4
It's a Small World 16 1-17
It's for My Valentine 220 7-27
It's in Your Hands 236 8-7
I've Gotta Crow 18 1-20

Jasmine Flower, The 58 2-31
Johnny, Get Your Hair Cut 251 8-33

Keep Your Eyes on the Prize 190 7-3
Knock the Cymbals 241 8-24

SONG INDEX

La raspa 84   3-24, 3-25
Land of the Silver Birch 260, 285   8-39
Let's Go to the Sea *(Vamos a la mar)* 294   9-12
Little Boy of the Sheep 64   2-37
Loco-Motion, The 80   3-19
Love Somebody 277   9-1
Lovely Hala Trees *(Nani Wale Na Hala)* 174
   6-14
Lullaby for the Trees 30   2-1

Make a Rainbow 128   5-4
Make New Friends 48   2-21
Maps and Globes 226   8-2
Market of San José, The *(En la Pulga de San
   José)* 170   6-11
May the Sun Shine Forever 70   3-8
Melchior and Balthazar 264   8-43
Morning Bells 246   8-28
My Home's in Montana 148   5-20
My Old Black Cat Hates Halloween 194   7-7

Never Gonna Be Your Valentine 222   7-28
Never Sleep Late Any More 275, 298   8-50
Never Smile at a Crocodile 154   5-25
New Year's Greeting, A 219   7-26
Now Let Me Fly 78   3-17
Now Sleep, Little Fellow *(Dormite, niñito)* 172
   6-13

Oh, Won't You Sit Down? 102   4-7
Old Aunt Dinah 244   8-26
Oleana 156   5-27

Paw Paw Patch 249   8-31
Peace like a River 56   2-29
Phoebe 255, 257   8-35
Piñata 212   7-21
Polly Wolly Doodle 104   4-10
Poor Little Kitty Cat 256   8-37
Pumpkin, Pumpkin 253   8-34

Ring, Bells 265   8-44
Rockin' Robin 8   1-6
Rocking Carol, The 210   7-18

Roll on the Ground 90   3-30
Rudolph, the Red-Nosed Reindeer 206   7-15

Sailboat in the Sky 176   6-15
Sandy Land 42   2-15
Save the Planet 114   4-20
Scotland's Burning 276   8-51
Shuckin' of the Corn 196   7-8
Skip to My Lou 43   2-17
Sleep Well, Little Children 208   7-17
Social Studies 224   8-1
Song of the Crow 292   9-10
Star-Spangled Banner, The 182   6-19
Stodola Pumpa 12   1-12
Sun and the Moon, The *(El sol y la luna)* 74
   3-13
Sweet Potatoes 92   3-31

Take Me Out to the Ball Game 22   1-24
Tender Shepherd 49   2-23
This Land Is Your Land 116   4-23
Tideo 247, 252   8-29
Tiny Boat, The *(El barquito)* 166   6-5
Turn the Glasses Over 72, 300   3-10
Two Wings 34   2-6

Walk Together, Children 122   4-27
We Come to Greet You in Peace 124   5-1
We've Got Lots in Common 4   1-1
Whaka Poi 52   2-25
Wheel of the Water, The 44   2-20
Winter Wonderland 202   7-11

Yankee Doodle 150   5-21
Yoop Biddy 289   9-7

Acknowledgments and Picture Credits

Acknowledgments

Credit and appreciation are due publishers and copyright owners for use of the following.

Exercise #6 of "Seven Little Instrumental Pieces" from Part I of Orff-Schulwerk MUSIC FOR CHILDREN, VOLUME II, edited by Margaret Murray. ©1959, renewed, by B. Schott's Soehne. All rights reserved. Used by permission of European American Music. (p. 32) Exercise 30 from Orff-Schulwerk MUSIC FOR CHILDREN, VOLUME I, edited by Margaret Murray. ©1959, renewed by B. Schott's Soehne. All rights reserved. Used by permission of European American Music. (p. 47) "My Father's Valentine" from IT'S VALENTINE'S DAY by Jack Prelutsky, © 1983, Scholastic Inc., New York. "No Rain, No Rainbow" from SAY IT AGAIN, GRANNY by John Agard. Published by The Bodley Head Ltd. Used by permission. "The Peace Dove," © Oceanna Chatard. Used by permission. "The Water-Go-Round" by Dennis Lee. Used by permission. "Weather" from CATCH A LITTLE RHYME by Eve Merriam. ©1966 by Eve Merriam. Used by permission of Marian Reiner for the author.

The editors of Silver Burdett Ginn Inc. have made every attempt to verify the source of "Goin' to the Party," "Great Big House," and "Song of the Crow," but were unable to do so. We believe them to be in the public domain.

Every effort has been made to locate all copyright holders of material used in this book. If any errors or omissions have occurred corrections will be made.

Photograph and Illustration Credits

All photographs are by Silver Burdett Ginn (SBG) unless otherwise noted.

Cover: Ken Bowser.
2. John Courtney. 4–5: Christopher Denise. 6–7: Rhonda Voo. 8–9: ill. Mary Thelen; photograph H. Armstrong Roberts. 10–11: Jack Graham. 12: © John Eastcott/Yva Momatiuk. 13: t.l. Mike Powell/Allsport Photographic Ltd.; t.r. Chris Pillitz/WestStock; m. © Duomo Photography, Inc.; b. Yahn Guichaoua/Agence Vandystadt/Allsport. 14: ill. Bernard Maisner; photograph Culver Pictures, Inc. 15: ill. Floyd Cooper; b. Jesse J. Santos. 16–17: Craig Smallish. 18–19: Karen Blessen. 20–21: Liisa Chauncy Guida. 22–23: ill. Karen Blessen; photograph Joseph Szkodzinski/The Image Bank. 24–25: Terry Powell. 26: Deborah Rediger. 27: © Archiv/Photo Researchers, Inc. 28–29: title, border, inset © Peter Grindley/FPG. 28: inset Larry Dale Gordon/The Image Bank. 30–31: © 1990 Darrell Gulin/Allstock. 33: Roseanne Kaloustian. 34: Karen Blessen. 36–37: © H.R. Bramaz/Allstock. 39: © Archiv/Photo Researchers, Inc. 40–41: ill. Kelly Hume; photograph David Noble/FPG; t. inset Mike Malyszko/Stock, Boston Inc.; m. inset © Brett Froomer/The Image Bank; b inset W. Hille/Leo deWys, Inc. 42: Elliott Varner Smith for SBG. 44–45: © Superstock, Inc.; border © Stephen Green-Armytage/The Stock Market. 46: Steve Salerno. 48–49: James Kirkland; border ill. Joann Adinolfi. 50–51: Deborah Healy. 51: © Topham/The Image Works. 52: David Wariner. 53: © Joe Viesti/Viesti Associates, Inc.; inset Lawrence Migdale for SBG. 54–55: © Superstock, Inc. 56–57: ill. Blake Thornton; photograph John Hicks/Leo deWys, Inc. 58–59: Joyce Protzman. 60–61: Denny Bonds; ill. inset David Diaz; photograph inset Courtesy Theodore Presser Company; title ill. Kelly Hume. 64–65: Steve Cieslawski. 66: Francisco Mora. 67: title ill. Francisco Mora. 68–69: © Eleanor Thompson/The Stock Market. 70: Jackie Besteman. 71: © FPG. 72–73: Elliott Varner Smith for SBG. 74–75: Fabriscio Breck. 76–77: Barbara Lambase. 77: Stock Montage, Inc. 78–79: Tony Craddock/Tony Stone Images; ill. Jennifer Hewittson. 80–81: Kelly Hume. 82: *Green Snake Quilt* by Susie Ponds, from the Collection of Maude Southwell Wahlman. 83: Jack Graham. 84–85: Donna Ingemanson. 86–87: ill. Ben Mahan; photographs Springer/Bettmann Film Archive; © Richard Hutchings/Photo Researchers, Inc. 88: © Craig Aurness Woodfin Camp & Associates, Inc. 90: Brock May/Photo Researchers, Inc. 91: Courtesy of The Oakland Museum, History Department. 92: Pat Alexander. 93: Doug Armand/Tony Stone Images. 96: ill. Kelly Hume; photograph Lawrence Migdale for SBG. 97: © Archive Photos/G.D. Hackett. 98–99: Ron Morecraft. 98: © Superstock. 99: © Herb Snitzer/Stock, Boston; Mercury Archives/The Image Bank; John Bacchus for SBG. 100–101: Robert Bryd. 102–103: Rhonda Voo. 104–105: ill. Dave Johnson; photographs Elliott Varner Smith for SBG. 106–107: backgrounds Jerry Pavey. 106: photographs t. Lara Hartley Photography; b. Peter Schaaf for SBG. 107: t. Peter Schaaf for SBG, b. Bob Winsett/Tom Stack & Associates. 108: Peter Schaaf for SBG. 109: Christian Steiner. 110–111: Pamela Harrelson. 110: © Jack Vartoogian. 111: t. © Catherine Karnow/Woodfin Camp & Associates, Inc.; b. Steve Vidler/Leo deWys, Inc. 112: Patti Boyd. 114–115: (Begin t.r. reading clockwise) S. Nielsen/IMAGERY; S. Nielsen/IMAGERY; Paul Rogers/IMAGERY; © Steven Stefanovic/Okapia/Photo Researchers, Inc.; © ColorBox 1992/FPG; Breck P. Kent; S. Nielsen/IMAGERY; © Pat & Tom Leeson/Photo Researchers, Inc.; Breck P. Kent; © Steve Maslowski/Photo Researchers, Inc.; © Robert Bornemann/Photo Researchers, Inc.; Breck P. Kent; ill. Frank McShane. 116–117: Jerry Pavey. 118–119: Susan Gal. 120–121: ill. Deborah Rediger; photographs (Begin t.l. reading clockwise) Chip Henderson/Tony Stone Images; Stephen Green-Armytage/The Stock Market; Ron Kimball; Pete Saloutos/The Stock Market; Ron Kimball; Ron Kimball; Ron Kimball; Ron Kimball. 122–123: Carol Simowitz. 124–125: Jack Stockman. 126–127: Renato Rotolo/Gamma Liaison Network; inset Elliott Varner Smith for SBG. 127: Renato Rotolo/Gamma Liaison Network. 128–129: Cindy Salans

Rosenhiem. 130–131: ill. Karen Blessen; photographs (Begin t.l. reading clockwise) Luis Villota/The Stock Market; David Hiser/Tony Stone Images; Ginny Ganong Nichols/Viesti Associates, Inc.; Reed Kaestner/Viesti Associates, Inc.; Lawrence Migdale/Tony Stone Images. 132–133: Lindsay Hebberd/Woodfin Camp & Associates, Inc. 134–135: Grant Heilman/Grant Heilman Photography; inset Smithsonian Institution, Alice Fletcher's Annual Report-Bureau of Ethnology 1900. 136–137: background photo John Running; title ill. Raphealle Goethals. 136: l. Theo Westenberger/Liaison USA; r. John Running. 137: Theo Westenberger/The Gamma Liaison Network. 138–139: © Adam Woolfitt/Woodfin Camp & Associates, Inc.; John Running. 140: The Shrine to Music Museum/University of South Dakota. 140–141: Robert & Linda Mitchell. 142–143: ill. Andrea Eberback; inset photographs t.r. Michael Ziegler for SBG; b.r. Ken Karp for SBG. 144–145: ill. Karen Blessen. 146–147: ill. Oliva Cole; photograph Dominique Braud/Tom Stack & Associates. 148–149: ill. Kelly Hume. 151: Elliott Varner Smith for SBG. 152–153: Liisa Chauncy Guida. 154–155: Darius Detwiler. 156–157: Liz Callen. 158–159: Wayne Vincent. 160–161: Gerardo Suzan. 162–163: Liz Callen. 164–165: Michael Ziegler for SBG. 166–167: Denise Fernando. 168–169: Fabricio Varden Broeck. 170–171: Joe Viesti/Viesti Associates, Inc. 172: ill. Kelly Hume; photographs W. Cody/WestLight; inset Mughsots/The Stock Market. 174–175: © Douglas Faulkner/Photo Researchers, Inc.; inset R.E. Pelham/Bruce Coleman, Inc. 176–177: Kim HeeYoung. 178–179: Jean Paul Nacivet/Leo deWys, Inc. 179: © Roland & Sabrina Michaud/Woodfin Camp & Associates, Inc. 180–181: George Hunter/Tony Stone Images. 182–183: Craig Hammell/The Stock Market. 184–185: Robin Hotchkiss. 186–187: Esther Baran. 188–189: Courtesy of Kim & Reggie Harris. 190–191: © James H. Karales; inset © Bob Adelman/Magnum Photos. 194–195: © Wlater Chandoha. 198–199: Tony Stone Images; insets E.R. Degginger/Color-Pic, Inc.; border David Sutherland/Tony Stone Images. 200–201: Jack Stockman. 202–203: © Gary Braasch/Woodfin Camp & Associates, Inc. insets t. Allen B. Smith/Tom Stack & Associates; m. John Shaw/Tom Stack & Associates; b. Allen B. Smith/Tom Stack & Associates. 203: inset Kristian Hilsen/Tony Stone Images. 204–205: Steve Salerno. 206–207: Steve Sanford. 208–209: Sandra Speidel. 210–211: © Zigy Kaluzny. 212–213: Rene Michael Trapega; border Nik Wheeler/Westlight. 214: Margaret Cusak. 215: David Diaz. 216–217: © Lawrence Migdale. 218–219: Tony Stone Images; inset Cameramann International, Ltd.; origami by Nancy Haffner; border Ken Straiton/The Stock Market. 221: Elliott Varner Smith for SBG. 222–223: Mary Thelan. 224–225: Robert Llewellyn; ill. Karen Blessen. 226–227: Thomas Winz/Panoramic Images. 228: © Peter B. Kaplan. 229: Brown Brothers. 230–231: J. Schwabel/Panoramic Stock Images; inset Frank P. Rossotto/The Stock Market. 232–233: Camerique/H. Armstrong Roberts, inset U.S. Dept of the Interior-National Park Service, Edison National Historic Site. 238: Maria Stroster. 240–241: John Berg. 242–243: Tom Leonard. 244: © Dwight Kuhn. 245: © Timothy O'Keefe/Southern Stock Photo Agency. 246–247: ill. Peter Lacalamita; photograph © Wolfgang Kaehler. 248–249: photograph © Kevin Shields/New England Stock Photo; ill. Tom Leonard. 250–251: Lyle Miller. 250: Courtesy of Country Music Foundation. 251: The Bettmann Archive. 252: ill. Arvis Stewart; photograph The Bettmann Archive. 253: ill. Arvis Stewart; photograph A.F. Accetta/FPG, inset Lawrence Migdale for SBG. 254–255: North Carolina State Archive. 254: ill. Sharon O'Neil. 256–257: Diane Patterson. 259: ill. Arvis Stewart; photograph Lawrence Migdale for SBG. 260: Alan Oddie/Photo Edit. 261: t. National Museum of African Art, photograph by Frank Khoury; b. National Museum of African Art, photograph by Frank Khoury. 262: inset & border Jerry Jacka Photography. 263: *Log Cabin Quilt* by Mozell Benson, from the collection of Maude Southwell Wahlman. 264: John T. Ward. 265: ill. John T. Ward. 266–267: Mary Beth Schwark. 268: Scott Angle. 270: Arvis Stewart. 272: Lawrence Migdale for SBG. 273: James Blank/Southern Stock Photos. 276: Wayne Aldridge/International Stock; t.r. Stock Montage, Inc. 277: ill. Frank McShane; photograph I. Benn Mitchell/The Image Bank; t.r. Charles Gupton/Stock, Boston; b.r. Richard Hutchings/Photo Edit. 279: Diane Blasius. 283: Rose Krans Hoffman. 284: ill. Diane Blasius; photograph © S.R. Maglione/Photo Researchers, Inc. 285: Mitchell Funk/The Image Bank. 286: ill. Tom Leonard; photograph E.R. Degginger/Picture Perfect USA. 287: ill. Tom Leonard. 288: ill. Christa Kieffer; photograph Courtesy of Anyone Can Whistle. 289: Jerry Jacka Photography; border Eric Simon/Stock, Boston. 290: Dara Goldman. 291: ill. Donald Gates; title ill. Rhonda Voo. 292–293: Michelle Lester. 294: Curt Shields/Southern Stock Photo Agency. 295: Willard Clay/FPG. 296: ill. Sarah Waldron; photograph Charles D. Winters/Stock, Boston. 298–299: Ken Cole/Animals Animals. 299: t.l. Richard Hutchings for SBG; t.r. © Peter Steiner/The Stock Market; b.l. Alfred Gescheidt/The Image Bank; b.r. © Len Rue, Jr./Stock, Boston. 300–301: ill. Daniel Morton

Sound Bank Photos 304: Bear Growler- Bryon Burton. 305: Wooden Flute-The Shrine to Music Museum/University of south Dakota. 306: Oud- The Shrine to Music Museum/University of South Dakota; Panpipes- Robert Houser for SBG. 307: Requinto- Courtesy Zazhil/Bill Albrecht for SBG.

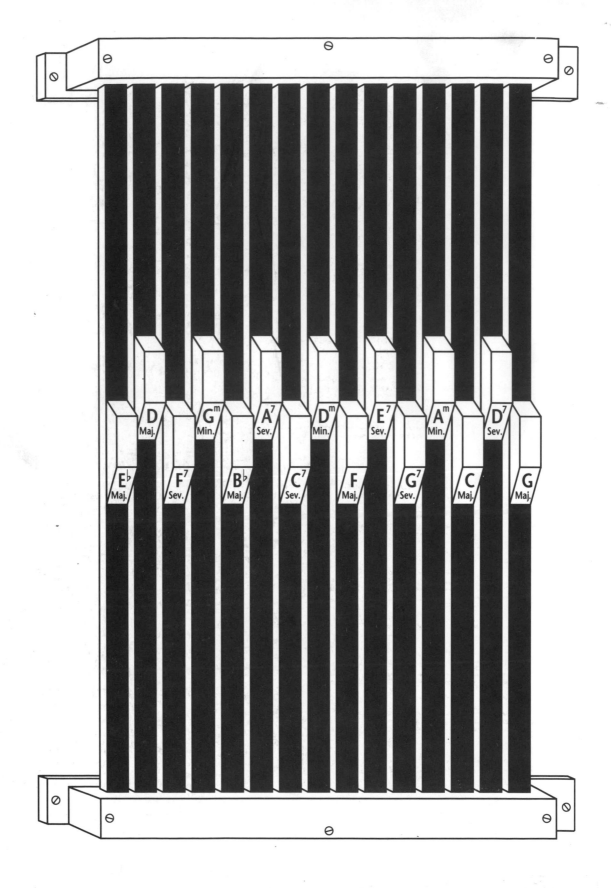